fondue

the essential kitchen

fondue

robert carmack

PERIPLUS

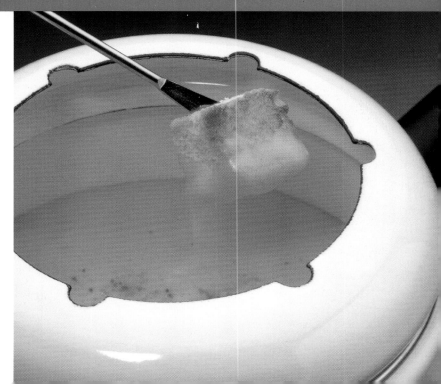

contents

fondue

introduction

Fondue has always been a communal affair. In the old days, though, people ate from one pot in the center of the table, without the niceties of plates and forks.

The Swiss elevated fondue to an art form, and its origin rests squarely in the Alps, particularly in the canton of Neuchâtel or Neuenburg. Today, fondue is a popular Swiss restaurant dish, particularly in ski areas. Waiters speedily supply bubbling fondue pots, known as *caquelons*, resting them on high standing trivets over a small alcohol flame. Chefs compete to produce the best fondue in the canton. And diners revel in afixing small bits of bread or other morsels onto the tips of long forks and immersing them into the tabletop cauldrons. *Cuisine à la minute* never had a more precise meaning.

The word *fondue* is French for "melted." And traditional Swiss fondue is made of a blend of cheeses melted with alcohol. But today, vegetables, fruits, meat, and seafood fondues are also popular. The Swiss divide fondue into five categories: cheese, Burgundian, Bacchus, Asian and chocolate. For Burgundian fondue, or *fondue bourguignonne*, raw meats and other foods are cooked at the table in a pot of rapidly simmering oil, then served with an array of dipping sauces. Bacchus fondue, named after the ancient god of wine, substitutes alcohol as the cooking medium, while chocolate fondue is a favorite for desserts. Asian fondues begin with either boiling water or broth, usually served in a distinct doughnut-shaped hot pot. Meat and vegetables are cooked at the table in the liquid, and the enriched broth is then served as a finale. This dish is variously known as a Mongolian hot pot, a firepot, or a steamboat.

Fondue, of course, is more than the liquid or sauce in the fondue pot. It is also the raw and blanched vegetables or cubed breads, meats, or fruits that are cooked or dipped in the fondue, as well as for dipping sauces and often salad to serve alongside. For example, a cheese fondue may be accompanied with pickled onions, boiled potatoes, and cucumbers, while Burgundian and Bacchus fondues are served with béarnaise sauce, mayonnaise, and condiments such as mustard, ketchup (tomato sauce), and chutney. Both fresh and dried fruits ideally accompany chocolate fondues, along with cookies such as macaroons, ladyfingers, and cubes of cake.

Whether fondue is Western or Asian in concept, sweet or savory, four to six people is the optimum number at a fondue dinner. More guests than that results in too many people reaching too far across the table into too small a pot. Each diner should be equipped with his or her own plate or bowl and, ideally, individual bowls of dipping sauce, allowing guests to "double dip" with impunity. While one fondue fork per person is adequate for a cheese fondue, meat fondues require a number of skewers, as meats take a while to cook—guests will want to cook several pieces of meat at a time. Small wire-mesh skimmers, chopsticks, and tongs also come in handy for retrieving errant pieces of food.

Cheese fondue

With cheese fondue, cubes of bread and sometimes pieces of boiled potato, vegetables, and cooked meats are dipped in a luscious cheese sauce. Ideally, a classic cheese fondue requires well-aged imported Swiss cheese such as Emmentaler or Gruyère. Most New World Swiss-style cheeses, however, are seldom sufficiently matured to make a classic fondue. Just as Cheddar is commonly available as mild, sharp, and extra sharp in English-speaking countries, Gruyère and Emmentaler come in varying degrees of pungency when sold in the Alps. The subtle blending of these different cheese flavors is a distinguishing characteristic of Swiss fondues.

In England, America, and other English-speaking countries, a wide assortment of cheeses can be used in melted-cheese dishes. England and colonial America both produced versions of rarebit, or rabbit, sometimes substituting strong ale or stout for Continental wines. Feta and other fresh sheep's- and goat's-milk cheeses, including blue-veined varieties, melt sufficiently when bound with either flour or cornstarch (cornflour). To make the nacho-like fondue spiked with chopped green chilies, Monterey Jack may be used as a substitute for the Mexican cheeses of asadero or queso Chihuahua. Mozzarella is also a suitable substitute.

Burgundian fondue

Burgundian fondue is actually Swiss in origin. The reason it's called Burgundian is peculiar. Although there appears to be no clear historical link between Burgundy and oil-bathed food cooked at the table, one anecdote is that a Swiss restaurateur had a restaurant in that part of France, and later, when he relocated to Switzerland, he coined the term "fondue bourguignonne." The closest similarity is when Mexicans refer to a dish as "Swiss" simply because it is cooked with cream, and when the English or the French call a style "Indian" because it is flavored with curry powder.

With Burgundian fondue, a metal pot (either stainless steel or cast iron) is best suited. Pieces of raw meat are cooked in simmering fat, then dipped in an assortment of dipping sauces. Since the meat cooks in a matter of minutes, it should be cubed from tender cuts: beef tenderloin; boneless, skinless chicken breast; pork and lamb tenderloin. The exception is flank steak (skirt steak), which is cut into thin slices. To use slow-cooking vegetables, parboil them in advance. Skewers are preferred to forks for Burgundian fondues, as they allow diners to pierce through the meat, letting the skewer protrude ½ inch (12 mm) at the other end. The skewer can then rest on the bottom of the pot, which keeps the meat from sticking to the pot.

Either oil, clarified butter, or ghee may be used as the cooking medium for a Burgundian fondue. Use a good-quality oil such as grapeseed or peanut, as these withstand high temperatures without smoking. Clarified butter also withstands frying temperatures without burning (see recipe page 105). Ghee, or Indian clarified butter, is an easy substitute, available in cans from any Asian or Indian grocer, and in the gourmet aisles of many supermarkets. Take special care when cooking with oil, melted butter or ghee at the table, as nasty burns occur from a single drop.

A typical Burgundian fondue comes with béarnaise sauce, mayonnaise and condiments such as mustard, ketchup (tomato sauce), and chutney. After cooking, the pieces of food are dipped into a spicy sauce, followed by a hot dip, followed by another sour, one sweet, and so on.

Bacchus fondue

Bacchus fondues use wine in place of oil. The same cuts of meat are used as for Burgundian fondues, but the meats are usually cut into thin strips and threaded onto skewers. Either a stoneware or a metal pot may be used. White wine is the classic cooking medium, which can be flavored with a bouillon cube or fresh herbs. Sherry, beer, and rice wine may also be used for cooking, but high-proof spirits may not, as they become flammable when heated.

Either fondue forks or skewers may be used to spear or thread the pieces of food. As with Burgundian fondue, after cooking the food is dipped into one or more sauces.

Asian fondue

Like Western fondue, the Asian hot pot began with a central heat source in a cold room. To conserve precious fuel, a pot of broth was set atop a brazier, and small pieces of food were cooked in the vessel.

Asian fondues have a plethora of names: hoh go, shabu shabu, lau, and sin sul lo. In the West, they are variously called Mongolian hot pots, firepots and steamboats. As in a Bacchus fondue, foods are cooked in a poaching liquid. Asian fondues, however, are traditionally cooked in a large, doughnut-shaped pot. The larger circumference of the pot allows for the simultaneous cooking of more foods than a smaller pot. Chopsticks and small wire-mesh skimmers are used to fish out the foods, which are then dipped into a sauce. The broth becomes richer with the addition of each meat and vegetable, and after all the pieces of food have been cooked and eaten, cooked rice or noodles are added to the concentrated broth, then ladled out into small bowls as a delicious finale.

The steaming liquid is the source for the name steamboat, while firepot takes its name from the smoking center chimney filled with hot coals. The pots are commonly made of brass and stainless steel, but inexpensive aluminum versions may be found on the market; electric models are also available. In all cases, it is essential to add the liquid before heating the pot; otherwise, the solder joins of the pot might melt from the heat of the coals. When using steamboats, ensure you place a heatproof trivet or brick beneath it on a tabletop. When burning charcoal indoors, make sure that the room is very well ventilated. Charcoal releases carbon monoxide, so if anyone at the table begins to feel drowsy, open the windows immediately.

Alternatives to hot pots include a metal fondue pot, or for more authenticity, a large pottery sand pot, chrysanthemum bowl, or Japanese donabe, set atop a raised trivet with an alcohol flame underneath. A wok sitting on a portable gas base also works well, but carbon steel woks tend to rust over long exposure to liquid; a nonstick or stainless steel wok is preferable here.

Chocolate fondue

Chocolate fondues arrived late on the scene, originating in the 1950s as a dish using Toblerone, a well-known Swiss brand. Reportedly the creation of a New York publicist for that chocolate company, the dish was then embraced by a Swiss restaurant in New York frequented by embassy staff and expatriates alike. When they, in turn, headed back to Europe, they introduced chocolate fondue to the Swiss nation, where it received a ready welcome. Always use a good grade of chocolate, preferably coverture, and melt it over low heat, to prevent burning. Steam and droplets of water must be avoided when melting chocolate, or it will seize into a stiff mass.

Suggested quantities for fondues

The amounts needed will depend on whether you are serving one or more kinds of food.

Cheese: 4-6 oz (125–185 g) per person; Meat: 8 oz (250 g) per person; Fish and shellfish (shelled): 6 oz (185 g) per person; Bread: 1 loaf per 2–3 persons, or about twenty 1-inch (2.5-cm) cubes per person;

Vegetables and fruit: 6–8 oz (185–250 g) per person (before trimming); Fruits, dried and fresh: about 2–4 oz (60–125 g) per person (before peeling and coring); Cookies (biscuits): about 4 per person;

Candy (confectionary): about 4–6 per person

Step-by-step cheese fondue

1 Cut a loaf of crusty bread into thick slices, then into bite-sized cubes about 1 inch (2.5 cm) square.

2 Dice or coarsely shred the cheese.

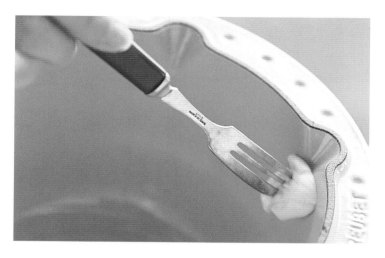

3 Rub the inside of a saucepan or fondue pot with a garlic clove. The garlic remnants may either be finely chopped and added to the pot, or discarded.

4 Heat the liquid, in this case wine and lemon juice, in a saucepan or as here, in a fondue pot. When the liquid is hot, reduce heat to low and add cheese.

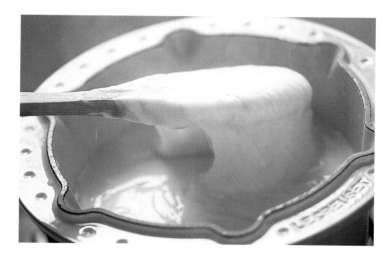

5 Stir in a figure-8 movement to melt the cheese. Do not melt too quickly over too high a heat, or cheese will become tough and stringy.

6 Dissolve potato flour or cornstarch (cornflour) in kirsch, vodka, or a similar distilled spirit. Stir into the fondue to bind and stabilize it, as well as to add flavor. Cook for a minute or two longer, adding ground pepper and freshly grated nutmeg.

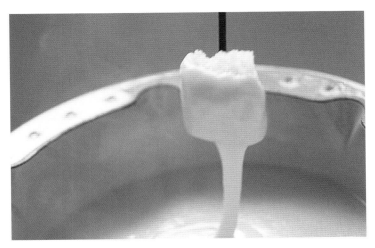

Melting cheeses

The most common Swiss cheeses for fondue are Emmentaler and Gruyère. Although varying in flavor, other cheeses that melt particularly well are English Lancashire and Cheshire cheeses; Italian fontina, provolone, and mozzarella; and American jack cheese. Although a common addition to melting blends, and an essential ingredient in rarebit, Cheddar curdles easily and becomes grainy. Many blue-veined cheeses melt reasonably well.

7   If the fondue has been prepared in a saucepan, warm a fondue pot and pour mixture into it. Serve at the table, over a raised trivet and alcohol flame. (Note: a candle flame is insufficient.) Spear bread cubes onto long-handled fondue forks and dip into the cheese, swirling to coat neatly and to prevent dripping. Eat directly from the fork.

Step-by-step Bacchus fondue

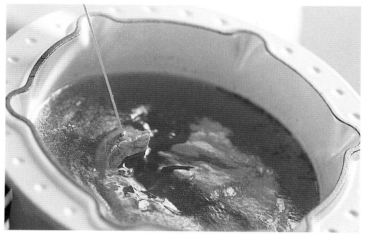

1   Pour just enough dry white wine into a fondue pot to fill by about two-thirds; heat to a rapid simmer. If desired, add 1 or 2 bouillon cubes for added flavor.

2   Thread a piece of vegetable or a meat strip on a skewer, plunge it into the simmering wine, and cook. Remove cooked food from the liquid, drain, then dip into an assortment of accompanying sauces.

Note: Because of wine's acidity, fondue pots made of stoneware or nonreactive metals should be used for Bacchus fondues. Don't use aluminum, and if using copper, make sure that it is well lined with tin, nickel, or stainless steel. Exposed patches of copper are toxic.

Step-by-step Burgundian fondue

1 Fill a metal fondue pot no more than one-third full with oil, preferably grapeseed or peanut oil. At the table, heat oil to 325–350°F (165–175°C), or until simmering. Once the oil is hot, do not move the pot.

2 Spear a piece of vegetable or meat with a skewer, pushing the skewer through so that it protrudes by $\frac{1}{2}$ inch (12 mm) at the other end. Skewer then rests on pan bottom, preventing food from touching the pot and sticking. Dip cooked food into one or more sauces. Let oil cool completely before removing pot from the table.

Cautions when cooking with oil, butter, or ghee

- While the traditional cheese fondue pot is made of stoneware, the high heat of simmering fat can crack this material. A cast iron or stainless steel pot is essential for Burgundian fondue.
- Be vigilant when deep-frying in the kitchen, and even more so when cooking at the table. When moist food comes in contact with hot oil, it literally explodes with vapor. For this reason, cook only a few pieces of food at a time. For tabletop deep-frying, use a slightly lower temperature than on a stove top. The oil should be gently simmering, not boiling.
- Never fill the pan more than one-third full of oil, butter, or ghee.
- Always stay close at hand when the fat is hot; never leave the pot unattended.
- Never shift or move a pot of hot fat.
- Remove skewers of food carefully from the oil to avoid dripping hot fat on the table or your partners.
- In case of a fire, do not douse with water. This can spread the flame. Instead, use a fire blanket or fire extinguisher.

Step-by-step Asian fondue

1   Light a small pile of lump or natural charcoal in a fireplace or in an outdoor grill. Natural charcoal is preferable to charcoal briquettes because it's pure and burns at a higher temperature. Mound the charcoal around an electric fire starter, plug it in, and after 7 minutes remove the starter. Alternatively, light charcoal in a charcoal chimney: tightly wad newspaper in its base, place charcoal on top, and set the newspaper alight. Do not use instant lighter liquids, firesticks, and other chemical fire agents, as these may produce unpleasant fumes at the table. Never use gasoline or kerosene, as both are dangerously explosive. Pour hot broth into a firepot or metal fondue pot to fill it by about two-thirds.

2   Once the coals are covered with a layer of white ash, after about 20 minutes, use long-handled metal tongs to transfer them into the chimney of the pot. Wear a heavy oven mitt in case some charcoal falls and requires quick retrieval. Add hot coals to the center of the chimney pot, filling it no more than halfway. Bring the broth to a rapid simmer.

(Note: if the pot has a lid attached to the chimney stack, remove it during cooking; cover to douse the flame. Conversely, many models have a ring lid for the stock; this should be in place to sufficiently raise the broth temperature prior to cooking.)

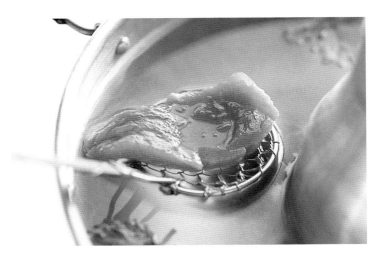

3 Use small wire-mesh skimmers, chopsticks, and tongs to dip raw foods into and retrieve cooked foods from the broth, and then dip them into the accompanying sauces. (Note: Wire-mesh skimmers come in a variety of sizes and are available in Asian markets and cookware stores, as are chopsticks and tongs. After guests have finished eating the meat and vegetables, add cooked rice or soaked noodles to the broth. Heat through and ladle into soup bowls. However, some broths, such as Vietnamese lau, are too pungent to eat as soup.

Cautions

Charcoal

- When burning any form of charcoal, always make sure that the room is well ventilated. Otherwise, carbon monoxide poisoning may occur.
- Never place a coal-heated pot directly on a table. It will char wood and melt plastic, and may shatter materials such as glass. Place the pot on a fireproof base such as bricks or a stone slab. If there is a likelihood that the heat will conduct through the bricks onto the table, place a fireproof mat under the base. (Note: Some electrical pots require similar measures.)

Raw eggs

- Some eggs, especially in the UK and North America, contain salmonella, which can be transmitted when eaten raw. Frustratingly, many Asian recipes for hot pots include raw egg as a dipping sauce. Its inclusion is therefore optional. Although not fool-proof, one solution to this problem is to avoid battery chicken eggs and purchase only eggs from free-range hens that have been organically fed. (Salmonella became endemic in factory chickens because they were fed reconstituted chicken parts.)

Chilies

- When working with chilies, avoid touching your skin, eyes, and nose. Fresh chilies contain volatile oils that can burn skin and tender membranes. Always wash your hands well in hot, soapy water after use, and scrub the chopping board and knife.

Step-by-step chocolate fondue

1 Finely chop chocolate into small pieces, about ¼ inch (6 mm). This allows the chocolate to melt evenly.

2 Combine liquids (here, cream and liqueur) in a double boiler or a saucepan over barely simmering water. Add the chocolate all at once and stir until chocolate is melted and combined with the liquid. (Note: Never attempt to melt the chocolate before adding liquid, as it may seize. Because chocolate burns easily, it should not be melted over a direct flame. Use a double boiler or a bowl, or place over barely simmering water. Melt milk chocolate at an even lower temperature. In the microwave, cook chocolate, uncovered, at 70 per cent for 1 minute at a time, or until it looks half melted; stir until smooth.)

3 Cut into bite-sized pieces. Peel, pit, or stem fresh fruit as necessary shortly before serving. Drain and pat dry canned fruits, before arranging on a platter. To avoid discoloration, sprinkle with lemon juice. Dried fruits are ideal.

4 Set a fondue pot over a candle flame or Bunsen burner to warm, but do not overheat or the chocolate will be scorched when it is added. Alternatively, rinse a fondue pot in hot water, dry carefully with a kitchen cloth and keep in a warm spot until needed. (Note: the pot must be absolutely dry before adding the chocolate or the chocolate will seize.) Then pour chocolate into the warmed fondue pot. Spear a piece of fruit with a fondue fork and dip into the melted chocolate. Cookies are best handled with the fingers.

Couverture and compound chocolate

For chocolate fondue, use the best chocolate available. Chocolate is commonly divided into two groupings: pure and compound. Couverture, which is the highest grade of pure chocolate, is also known as dipping chocolate and is made from cocoa liqueur and cocoa butter. The more cocoa mass it contains, the darker (and more expensive) it becomes. (Semisweet and bittersweet chocolates fall under this category, but unsweetened chocolate is not suited for these recipes). By contrast, compound (or less-expensive) chocolate, which includes most chocolate chips, is made of cocoa powder, plus flavorings and stable vegetable fats. As its name implies, milk chocolate is dark chocolate diluted with milk. Because of this dilution, it is slightly cheaper. White chocolate is not really chocolate at all, although it is made from cocoa butter, plus milk, sugar, vanilla and lecithin.

The cheese

In Switzerland, the proprietary home of fondue, the most common cheeses used are Emmentaler, Gruyère, and Fribourg vacherin, while sometimes Appenzeller is substituted. Emmentaler, from the canton of Emmenthal, is the holey cheese known around the world as "Swiss cheese." Sadly, much of the world's product would not be recognized by a Swiss. Its facsimiles around the world are distant both in geography and taste. Mild Jarlsberg from Norway is a notable exception. Gruyère, which comes from the foothills of the Swiss Alps, is a hard cheese of similar appearance, but without the dominant holes. Confusingly, the term Gruyère has been appropriated by the French to refer generically to firm mountain cheeses like Comté, Beaufort, and Emmental. Strictly speaking, Gruyère hails only from La Gruyère district in Switzerland. Adding further puzzlement to the issue is vacherin. This firm, creamy-tasting cheese resembles Gruyère, but tastes less savory. Confusingly, a like-named cheese, Vacherin Mont d'Or, is not interchangeable with Fribourg vacherin, also known as vacherin fribourgeois. One variety of Vacherin Mont d'Or is rich and runny like a ripe Brie and, when at its peak, is covered with a snowlike mold delightful to the eyes as well as the mouth. Most of these cheeses are available through cheese stores, and many also have New World versions. Unfortunately, it is the variance in flavor due to the aging of these cheeses that cannot easily be found outside of Switzerland.

Besides Swiss cheeses, packs of generically labeled "pizza cheese" or "melting cheese" are readily available in supermarkets; many are preshredded. Because of the large portion of Cheddar in many of these blends, they are unreliable for smooth melting in a fondue. A better alternative is preshredded mozzarella. All of these cheeses are somewhat bland, lacking any particular flavor. To counter this blandness, you may wish to flavor them with assertive and piquant condiments like mustard and horseradish, diced pickles, and spices. Blue-veined cheeses melt reasonably well, but their taste is strong. Parmesan and brined cheeses like feta all require special treatment, as they easily separate into oil and solids when heated. They generally require a binding of flour or cornstarch (cornflour). Otherwise, begin with a thin white sauce, or béchamel, then melt in just enough of the desired cheese for flavor.

Bread, wine and liquor

Bread

A crusty loaf, such as a baguette, is the ideal bread for cheese fondue. Bread should be dense-textured and firm enough to slice neatly, but not stale. Sourdough, Italian ciabatta, or any crusty country loaf will work well. Whole-grain breads are also suitable, but make sure the bread is firm enough to skewer securely onto a fondue fork. Soft presliced white and whole-wheat bread is not suitable, except when toasted. (Note that when crusty bread is stored in plastic wrap, it becomes leathery and tough, rather than crisp.)

Wine and liquor

Dry white acidic wines are most suited to cheese fondue, because the acid helps to prevent lumps. You may also add 1 teaspoon lemon juice per $\frac{1}{3}$ cup wine to reinforce this tartness. Old-world wines, such as very dry Riesling or Italian Frascati, are suitable here, but floral New World wines rich in fruit, such as Chenin Blanc, oaky Chardonnay, and some Sauvignon Blancs, are less ideal. Similarly, a dry (hard) cider may be used, but again, most New World cider tends to be sweet and fruity. Beer, ale, porter, and stout are used in some recipes. Red wine is not traditionally used in fondues, or even served at a fondue dinner.

Wines and spirits used in Bacchus fondues are more variable, although generally dry by tradition. Sherry, Asian rice wines, even beer, ale, and stout may be used. The only restriction is alcohol content. Spirits are likely to catch fire when heated, and therefore should not be used.

Kirsch, a clear cherry distillate, is the most common liquor used in cheese fondue. Known as eaux-de-vie, similar spirits are distilled from a plethora of fruits: plum, peach and raspberries, just to name a few. Suitable replacements include neutral vodka, caraway-imbued aquavit from Scandinavia, or even juniper-flavored gin. Besides adding flavor to cheese fondue, kirsch is also drunk during the meal, when it is called *le coup du milieu*, or "the mid-meal shot." Traditionally, it is drunk from miniature fondue pots, although any liqueur glass will suffice. It is best consumed at a cool room temperature. Kirsch aficionados are wont to dip their bread into a glass of liqueur prior to dipping it into the fondue pot.

Vegetable platters

Attractively arranged vegetable platters may accompany any sort of savory fondue, whether cheese, Asian, Bacchus, or Burgundian. The key is whether the vegetable needs cooking prior to serving, or if a raw crunch is preferred.

In cheese fondues, vegetables are not cooked in the pot and may consequently require prior blanching. Broccoli and cauliflower florets; carrot, celery, and turnip sticks; and mushrooms may all be dunked raw, or alternatively blanched briefly to soften. Harder vegetables, especially root vegetables like potatoes, parsnips, and rutabagas (Swedes), require complete cooking before dipping into a cheese melt. Do not overcook them, however, or they might disintegrate.

Bacchus and Burgundian fondues, on the other hand, actually cook vegetables at the table. In this case, parboiling is required only to shorten the actual cooking time at the table, or to prevent discoloration; root vegetables should be parboiled for 1–3 minutes.

Vegetables for Asian hot pots are rarely precooked, as all the food is cooked at the table. The large, round doughnut shape of the pot is designed to hold more foods than would fit in a fondue pot. A typical selection includes Chinese napa cabbage, bok choy, bell pepper (capsicum) strips, and daikon. Even leafy greens such as spinach and mustard greens work well here, especially as these vegetables are fished out with a small wire-mesh skimmer, as opposed to a fork. On a more exotic note, edible chrysanthemum leaves are available at Asian grocers. They should be cooked very briefly to keep them from becoming bitter. Packaged tofu should be soaked in fresh water for 20 minutes prior to using. Soft, as opposed to firm, tofu is usually served here. Don't overcook tofu, merely heat through and retrieve with wire-mesh skimmers.

VEGETABLE PLATTERS

Fruit platters

Practically any firm fresh or dried fruit is suitable for a chocolate fondue, but a typical platter accompanying a dessert fondue might also include candied fruits, plus a selection of cookies, such as ladyfingers, macaroons, and vanilla wafers.

When preparing fresh fruits, orchard favorites like pears and apples should be cored and cut into thick slices, with peeling optional. Discoloration is a concern, however, so assemble platters at the last minute. These fruits benefit from acidulated water, to prevent darkening. Either soak them briefly in a pot of cold water spiked with 1/3 cup (3 fl oz/90 ml) lemon juice or vinegar per quart (liter), or lightly rub lemon juice over them. Likewise, peeled bananas, cut into large chunks, also discolor with time. Either brush bananas with lemon juice or rub with the exposed flesh of a cut lemon.

Stone fruits should be firm and not overripe. Mangos and papayas must be peeled, but not so nectarines. Grapes and strawberries are ideal, but raspberries and blackberries are too delicate, while gooseberries and cranberries are too tart and currants and blueberries too small. Melons should be peeled and seeded, then cut into cubes or shaped into balls with a melon baller. Peel kiwi fruit and cut into large chunks. In the citrus family, tangerines and mandarins are excellent, because they divide cleanly into sections. Lemons and limes are too tart, but candied kumquats are delicious. Dried fruits like figs and dates are welcome additions to fruit platters, as are candied and glacéed fruits. When in season use fresh pineapple, although canned pineapple chunks—either in natural juice or syrup—may be more convenient. Most other canned fruits, outside of lichees, are too soft. When dipping canned fruits in chocolate, make sure that they are patted dry first.

Some ideal combinations blend fruit and cheese, such as tart apples with sharp (tasty) Cheddar, and pears with blue cheese. Cooking fruit in a Burgundian fondue is slightly less practicable, as the fruit is likely to overcook and turn to mush.

Meat platters

Raw meats

Raw meats and seafood may be cooked in Bacchus, Burgundian, and Asian fondues. They should be attractively arranged, covered, and refrigerated until ready to use. As a rule of thumb, meat that is to be fried in oil is cut into small dice about ¾ inch (2 cm), but thin strips are preferred for Bacchus fondue, as the cooking is slightly slower. Asian fondues generally call for even thinner strips, or in the case of tougher cuts, matchsticks.

In commercial establishments, health regulators commonly require separate chopping boards for preparation of different meats, to reduce the risk of cross-contamination in foods. For this reason, you may wish to put different raw meats—that is, shellfish, beef, pork, and chicken—on separate platters or plates. Vegetables and fruits may safely be grouped together.

Generally speaking, marinated meats may either be drained and arranged on a platter, or more conveniently, kept in the marinade. In either case, guests skewer or thread pieces from the platter or dish. If guests must touch raw meats with their hands, set finger bowls at the table: soup bowls of warm water with a lemon round; accompany with small hand towels or cloth napkins.

Cooked meats

An array of cured cooked meats, from ham to pastrami and corned beef to dried sausages and smoked chicken and turkey, are appropriate accompaniments to a fondue. Cut them into bite-sized cubes and serve. Because these meats do not need additional cooking, they are suited to cheese fondues, and as they require only brief heating, are perfect for a quick plunge into wine, oil, or broth. Uncured cooked meats, such as roast pork, beef, and chicken, may also be diced and served, but they tend to overcook, especially in the case of Burgundian fondue.

Slicing meat, step-by-step

1. Beef, pork, and lamb prepared for Asian fondues should be cut paper-thin. Always cut across the grain to achieve more tender results. Many cooks prefer to slightly freeze the meat before cutting, making it easier to cut into thin slices. This, however, adversely affects the texture of the meat. The best results are with a meat slicer. Alternatively, wrap meat very tightly in plastic wrap and chill thoroughly. Place meat on a chopping board and hold it securely with your left hand. With your other hand, use a very sharp chef's knife to slice through the plastic, cutting the meat paper-thin.
2. Lay slices in a single layer on a platter slightly overlapping. Cover with plastic wrap and chill until ready to serve.

Caution

Rare meat: In industrialized countries, meat is regularly checked by health inspectors, so that the consumption of rare beef is relatively safe. However, there have been cases of toxoplasmosis, parasitic diseases, bacterial contamination such as e-coli, and recently mad-cow disease. Avoid serving any raw and undercooked meats to the aged or infirm, the very young, pregnant women, and those with an immune deficiency. Generally, solid pieces of hind quarter meat, as opposed to ground (minced) meat from the fore quarter, is much less at risk. Pork is historically cooked well done because of trichinosis, although this is less a concern today.

MEAT PLATTERS

fondues

Classic Neuchâtel fondue

1 clove garlic

1 cup (8 fl oz/250 ml) dry white wine

10 oz (300 g) Emmentaler cheese, diced
 or shredded

10 oz (300 g) Gruyère cheese, diced or shredded

1 1/2 tablespoons potato flour or cornstarch
 (cornflour) mixed with 1/4 cup (2 fl oz/60 ml)
 kirsch

1/4 teaspoon ground white pepper

pinch of freshly grated nutmeg

crusty bread, cut into cubes, for serving

Rub a medium, heavy saucepan with garlic. Either discard garlic pieces or finely chop them and add to the saucepan. Place pot over medium-high heat, add wine and bring just to a boil. Immediately reduce heat to low and add cheese, stirring slowly in a figure-8 pattern until cheese is just melted. It should melt very slowly—about 5 minutes in all—otherwise, it may become stringy and tough. Add potato flour or cornstarch mixture, pepper, and nutmeg to the cheese mixture. Simmer for about 2 minutes more. The fondue should gently sputter, not boil. (The fondue should be thick enough to just cover the bread; it will thicken at the table.)

Pour the fondue into a warmed fondue pot and serve immediately. At the table, guests should take several cubes of bread onto their plates, skewer one with a fork, and dip it into the pot, twirling gently to prevent drips. Eat directly from the fork.

Serves 4–6

Suggested quantities

Bread: 1 loaf per 2–3 persons, or about twenty
1-inch (2.5-cm) cubes per person

CLASSIC NEUCHÂTEL FONDUE

Swiss fondue variations

The mildest-tasting fondue is made solely of Emmentaler cheese. For a medium-flavored fondue, combine half Emmentaler and half Gruyère. Stronger yet is the blending of one-third Emmentaler and two-thirds Gruyère, while the most pungent fondue is made from only well-matured Gruyère. Following are some other famed Swiss variations.

Jura: Finely chop 2 shallots (French shallots) and sauté in 1 tablespoon butter until soft. Add wine and continue as in the master recipe.

Vaud: Finely chop 2 garlic cloves, add to the wine, and proceed as in the master recipe.

Appenzell: Substitute hard (dry) cider for the wine, and use equal quantities grated Appenzeller and Fribourg vacherin instead of Emmentaler and Gruyère.

Fribourg: Use only Fribourg vacherin, either young or very aged, and melt it in $\frac{1}{3}$ cup (3 fl oz/90 ml) hot water. No wine or kirsch is used here, on any flour or cornstarch (cornflour). Instead of bread cubes, serve with chats (small potatoes) boiled in their jackets. (Note: This fondue burns easily, so be sure to use very low heat.)

Glarus: Delete the wine. Melt 4 tablespoons (2 oz/60 g) butter in a saucepan and add 2 tablespoons flour. Stir over medium-low heat for 2 minutes, taking care not to brown. Add 10 oz (300 g) each shredded Gruyère and Sapsago (Schabzieger cheese), stirring until melted. Proceed as in the master recipe.

Tip: If the fondue is too thin, add more cheese. If too thick, add more wine.

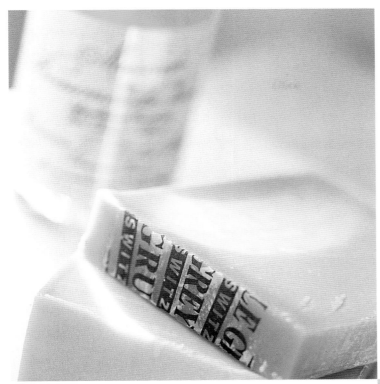

Green fondue with fresh herbs

1 small clove garlic

1 cup (8 fl oz/250 ml) medium-dry white wine

1 tablespoon fresh lemon juice

1¼ lb (625 g) Edam or Gouda cheese, shredded

1 tablespoon potato flour or cornstarch
  (cornflour)

¼ cup (¼ oz/7 g) chopped fresh parsley

2 tablespoons chopped fresh chives

2 teaspoons dried tarragon

pinch of cayenne pepper

½ teaspoon ground white pepper

1 tablespoon gin

slices of crusty bread, raw vegetables, and cooked
  meats of choice, for serving

Rub a medium, heavy saucepan with garlic clove. Add wine and bring just to a boil. Add lemon juice, and immediately lower heat to medium-low. Toss cheese with the potato flour or cornstarch, then add it to the pot handful by the handful, stirring with each addition until just melted. Add herbs, seasonings, and gin. Cook for 2–3 minutes, then transfer to a warmed fondue pot. Serve with the bread, vegetables, and meats alongside.

Serves 4–6

Suggested quantities

Meat: 8 oz (250 g) per person

Bread: 1 loaf per 2–3 persons, or about twenty 1-inch (2.5-cm) cubes per person

Vegetables: 6–8 oz (185–250 g) per person (before trimming)

GREEN FONDUE WITH FRESH HERBS

Pizza on a stick

2 tablespoons butter

2 tomatoes, peeled, seeded and chopped

1 large clove garlic, finely chopped

1 small onion, finely chopped

1/2 cup (4 fl oz/125 ml) dry white wine

2 teaspoons fresh lemon juice

1 lb (500 g) shredded mozzarella cheese

1 tablespoon potato flour or cornstarch
  (cornflour)

2 tablespoons capers, drained

2 anchovy fillets, coarsely chopped (optional)

1/2 teaspoon red chili pepper flakes, or to taste

1/2 teaspoon dried oregano

1 teaspoon salt

about 15 black olives, pitted and coarsely
  chopped

cubes of crusty bread, for serving

pepperoni or other dried sausages, cut into
  3/4-inch (2-cm) slices, and pineapple chunks,
  for serving (optional)

Melt butter in a heavy, medium saucepan over medium-high heat. Add tomatoes, garlic, and onion. Cook until onion is translucent, about 3 minutes. Add wine and lemon juice and reduce heat to low. Meanwhile, dust the cheese with the potato flour or cornstarch, then stir cheese in until melted and smooth, about 5 minutes.

Add capers and optional anchovies to the melted cheese. Stir in red pepper flakes, oregano and salt, and cook for 1–2 minutes. Transfer to a warmed fondue pot and top with olives. Serve with bread cubes, and if desired, sausage and pineapple. Secure them on fondue forks and dip into the fondue.

Serves 4–6

Variation

For a stronger blend, replace 4 oz (125 g) of the mozzarella with the same amount of grated Parmesan.

Suggested quantities

Meat: 8 oz (250 g) per person

Bread: 1 loaf per 2–3 persons, or about twenty 1-inch (2.5-cm) cubes per person

Fruit: 6–8 oz (185–250 g) per person (before peeling and coring)

PIZZA ON A STICK

Crab and Cheddar fondue

³/₄ cup (6 fl oz/180 ml) hard (dry) cider or beer

1 tablespoon fresh lemon juice

pinch of sugar

1 lb (500 g) sharp (tasty) Cheddar cheese,
  shredded

2 tablespoons all-purpose (plain) flour

7 oz (220 g) fresh lump crabmeat, picked over for
  shell

1 teaspoon caraway seed, lightly toasted

¹/₂ teaspoon salt, or to taste

pinch of cayenne pepper

cubes of crusty bread, for serving

In a double boiler over simmering water, heat the cider or beer, lemon juice, and sugar. Meanwhile, toss cheese with the flour. When liquid is hot, reduce heat, gradually stir in cheese, and let it melt slowly, about 5 minutes. Meanwhile, heat crabmeat in a microwave on medium high until warm, about 30 seconds. (This helps prevent the cheese from curdling later.) Add crabmeat, caraway seed, salt, and cayenne to the melted cheese. Transfer to a warm fondue pot and serve with the bread cubes alongside.

Serves 4–6

Suggested quantities

Bread: 1 loaf per 2–3 persons, or about twenty 1-inch (2.5-cm) cubes per person

CRAB AND CHEDDAR FONDUE

Fondue Mexicana

1 cup (8 fl oz/250 ml) beer

1 tablespoon fresh lemon juice

6 small fresh chilies, seeded and coarsely chopped

1/2 bell pepper (capsicum), seeded and diced

1 lb (500 g) Monterey jack or mild mozzarella
cheese, shredded

2 tablespoons all-purpose (plain) flour

1/2 teaspoon paprika

pinch of ground cumin

1 teaspoon salt, or to taste

tortilla chips, for serving

In a heavy, medium saucepan, heat beer over high heat until it foams. Add lemon juice, chilies and bell pepper. Reduce heat to medium. Toss cheese with the flour, paprika, and cumin, then add to the pan, 1 handful at a time, stirring to melt each handful. Add salt. Transfer to a warm fondue pot. Serve with the tortilla chips alongside.

Serves 4–6

Note: Wash your hands, knife and, chopping board well with hot, soapy water after touching the chilies, as their lingering oils will burn the skin.

Variation

One medium tomato, peeled, seeded and chopped may be added to the fondue at the same time as the bell pepper (capsicum).

FONDUE MEXICANA

Piedmont fonduta

1¹/₄ lb cold (625 g) Italian fontina cheese, thinly sliced

1 cup (8 fl oz/250 ml) milk

1 cup cream (if available, substitute 2 cups (16 fl oz/500 ml) half-and-half (half cream) for the cream and milk)

4 tablespoons (2 oz/60 g) butter at room temperature

6 egg yolks, lightly beaten

1 white truffle, thinly sliced or 1–2 tablespoons truffle oil (optional)

slices of crusty bread or cooked rice, for serving (optional)

Lay cheese slices in a 4-cup (32-fl oz/1-L) bowl, overlapping them slightly. Pour the milk and cream over the cheese. Let stand for at least 2 hours, or overnight. When ready, drain the cream and milk and measure out ½ cup (4 fl oz/125 ml). In a small saucepan, heat the cream and milk over low heat until bubbles form around the edges of the pan. Stir in the butter.

Put cheese in a double boiler over simmering water and stir constantly until melted. Gradually stir in the cream and milk until smooth and creamy. Gradually beat in egg yolks. The mixture should thicken slightly. Immediately transfer to a warmed fondue pot. If using, scatter the truffle slices or drizzle the truffle oil on top.

At the table, skewer bread slices onto forks and dip into the fondue, or spoon the fondue over individual bowls of rice to eat with a table fork. Because of this dish's egg content, it should be maintained over a very low flame and eaten immediately.

Serves 4–6

Suggested quantities

Bread: 1 loaf per 2–3 persons, or about twenty 1-inch (2.5-cm) cubes per person

½–1 cup cooked rice per person

PIEDMONT FONDUTA

Feta cheese melt

4 tablespoons (2 oz/60 g) butter

$^1/_4$ cup (2 fl oz/60 ml) olive oil

8 oz (250 g) feta cheese crumbled (about 1$^1/_2$ cups)

1 cup (8 fl oz/250 ml) milk, scalded

2 tablespoons potato flour or cornstarch
(cornflour) mixed with 2 tablespoons water

6 oz (180 g) canned crabmeat or shrimp (prawns),
drained

pita (pocket) bread, cucumber slices, pickles, and
marinated eggplant, for serving

In a small, heavy saucepan, melt butter with the oil over medium heat. Add cheese, stirring until melted. It will be creamy, but not smooth. Stir in milk, cooking until mixture is mostly smooth. Stir in the flour or cornstarch mixture. Cook until thickened, 1–2 minutes. Stir in the crabmeat or shrimp and transfer to a warmed fondue pot. Preheat broiler (grill). Just before serving, place the fondue pot under the broiler for about 2 minutes. Tear the bread into strips, roll, and skewer. Serve cucumber, pickles, and eggplant alongside.

Serves 4

Note: Sheep's-milk feta melts more easily than cow's, but both work well here. If the feta is too salty, soak it briefly in fresh water prior to using.

Variation

Substitute dry white wine for the milk.

Suggested quantities

Pita bread: 2–3 per person, depending on size of bread

Vegetables: 6–8 oz (185–250 g) per person (before trimming)

FETA CHEESE MELT

Blue cheese fondue

¹/₂ cup (4 oz/125 g) unsalted butter

2 shallots (French shallots), very finely chopped

1 clove garlic, finely chopped

1 cup (8 fl oz/250 ml) dry white wine

1 lb (500 g) blue cheese, crumbled

3 egg yolks

¹/₂ cup (4 fl oz/125 ml) Enriched meat stock,
  heated (see page 105)

¹/₂ teaspoon dried tarragon

1 tablespoon Dijon mustard

¹/₄ teaspoon salt

¹/₄ teaspoon ground pepper

rye bread and/or sourdough bread cubes, gherkins
  or cornichons, and pickled onions, for serving

In a medium, heavy saucepan, melt butter over medium-low heat. Sauté shallots and garlic until translucent, about 3 minutes. Add white wine, increase heat to medium and cook to reduce to a glaze, about 20 minutes. Sit the pan over a pot of simmering water. Stir in cheese until melted. Whisk egg yolks with the hot stock, then stir briskly into the melted cheese; add remaining ingredients. Continue cooking until slightly thickened; do not overcook or boil, or it may curdle. Immediately strain into a warm fondue pot and place over very low heat to keep warm. Serve with bread and pickles.

Serves 4–6

Suggested quantities

Bread: 1 loaf per 2–3 persons, or about twenty 1-inch (2.5 cm) cubes per person

BLUE CHEESE FONDUE

Welsh rarebit

$^1/_2$ cup (4 oz/125 g) butter

$^1/_2$ cup (4 fl oz/125 ml) beer or ale

1 lb (500 g) extra sharp (extra tasty) Cheddar or
  Lancashire cheese, shredded

salt to taste

$^1/_2$ teaspoon ground white pepper

1–2 loaves toasted bread slices, each cut into 4
  triangles, for serving

In a medium saucepan, combine butter and beer or ale. Heat over medium heat until bubbles appear. Reduce heat to medium low and add the cheese all at once, stirring until just melted. Add salt and pepper. Pour into a warmed fondue pot. Serve with toast. Use either forks or fingers to dip the bread.

Serves 4–6

Hint

For a richer rarebit, add 2 tablespoons bacon fat

with a similar amount of butter.

Stout rabbit

3/4 cup (6 oz/180 g) butter

2/3 cup (5 fl oz/150 ml) stout or porter

1 tablespoon all-purpose (plain) flour

1 lb (500 g) Stilton or blue cheese, crumbled

1 tablespoon prepared English (hot) mustard

1/2 teaspoon ground white pepper

1–2 loaves thin French bread, thinly sliced and
  toasted, for serving

In a medium saucepan, combine butter and stout or porter. Heat over low heat to melt the butter. Whisk in flour, then gradually add the cheese a little at a time, stirring just until melted. Add mustard and pepper. Pour into a warmed fondue pot. Serve with toast squares, using either fingers or a fork to dip the bread.

Serves 4–6

Raclette

about 1¼ lb (625 g) raclette cheese, in one wedge

about 1¾ lb (28 oz/875 g) small new potatoes
  (chats), boiled in their jackets

gherkins or cornichons, and pickled onions,
  for serving

Place 4 dinner plates in a very low oven to warm. Place cheese on a clean cutting board and set before an open fire. When cheese bubbles and melts, scrape it off with a wide palette knife and immediately spread it onto warm plates to eat immediately. Repeat as the cheese continues to melt.

Use potatoes to scrape up the cheese and eat with gherkins and onions.

Serves 4

Variation

Preheat oven to 450°F (230°C/Gas 8). Lay thin slices—about ⅛ inch (3 mm)—of cheese on individual ramekins or small ovenproof plates that have been lightly brushed with olive oil or butter. Heat in the oven until just melted, about 5 minutes. Serve immediately.

A fondue of marinated meats

3 lb (1.5 kg) beef rib eye steak (Scotch fillet), trimmed

FOR MARINADE

3 tablespoons white wine vinegar

$^1/_4$ cup (2 fl oz/60 ml) olive or good-quality salad or vegetable oil

$^1/_4$ cup (2 fl oz/60 ml) dry white wine

1 clove garlic, crushed

1 shallot (French shallot), finely chopped

1 teaspoon salt

2 teaspoons coarsely ground pepper

vegetable crudités of choice

4–5 cups (32–40 fl oz/1–1.25 L) dry white wine

Mounted béarnaise sauce (see page 102) or other dipping sauces of choice

crusty bread and green salad, for serving

Cut beef into thin strips. Combine marinade ingredients in a shallow dish and toss with the beef. Cover and refrigerate for at least 2 hours or overnight.

Place vegetables on a platter; cover and refrigerate until ready to bring to the table. Fill a stoneware or metal fondue pot two-thirds full with the wine. At the table, bring just to a rapid simmer. (Alternatively, measure the required amount, heat on the stove, and transfer to the fondue pot.) Drain beef and place it in a shallow serving dish. Thread meat on skewers and spear the vegetables, letting the end of each skewer protrude by $^1/_2$ inch (12 mm). Cook the meat 2–3 minutes, and the vegetables 3–5 minutes. Remove from the wine and dip into individual bowls of sauce. Accompany with crusty bread and green salad.

Serves 4–6

Suggested quantities

Bread: 1 loaf per 2–3 persons, or about twenty 1-inch (2.5-cm) cubes per person

Vegetables: 6–8 oz (185–250 g) per person (before trimming)

Variation

Substitute Aromatic oil marinade (see page 104) for the wine marinade.

La Gitana

2 lb (1 kg) boneless, skinless chicken breasts

1 lb (500 g) veal or pork tenderloin

1 teaspoon salt (optional)

vegetable crudités of choice

4–5 cups (32–40 fl oz/1–1.25 L) dry sherry

1–2 beef bouillon (stock) cubes (optional)

Mounted béarnaise sauce (see page 102) and
  Anchovy sauce (see page 103), or dipping sauces
  of choice

Slice chicken into thin strips. Cut veal into ¾-inch (2-cm) pieces; cut pork slightly smaller. Arrange meats on separate platters and lightly salt the pork, if using; cover and refrigerate. Arrange vegetables on a separate platter, cover, and refrigerate until ready to use.

Fill a stoneware or metal fondue pot about two-thirds full with the sherry and add bouillon cube(s), if using. At the table, heat to a rapid simmer. (Alternatively, measure the required amount, heat on the stove, and transfer to the fondue pot.) Secure meat onto wooden skewers, letting the end of the skewer protrude by ½ inch (12 mm). Plunge meat into the pot and cook for 3–7 minutes (chicken, veal and pork should not be rare). Repeat with vegetables, cooking until desired doneness. Serve with individual bowls of sauce.

Serves 4–6

Note: La Gitana takes its name from a Spanish sherry.

Suggested quantities

Vegetables: 6–8 oz (185–250 g) per person (before trimming)

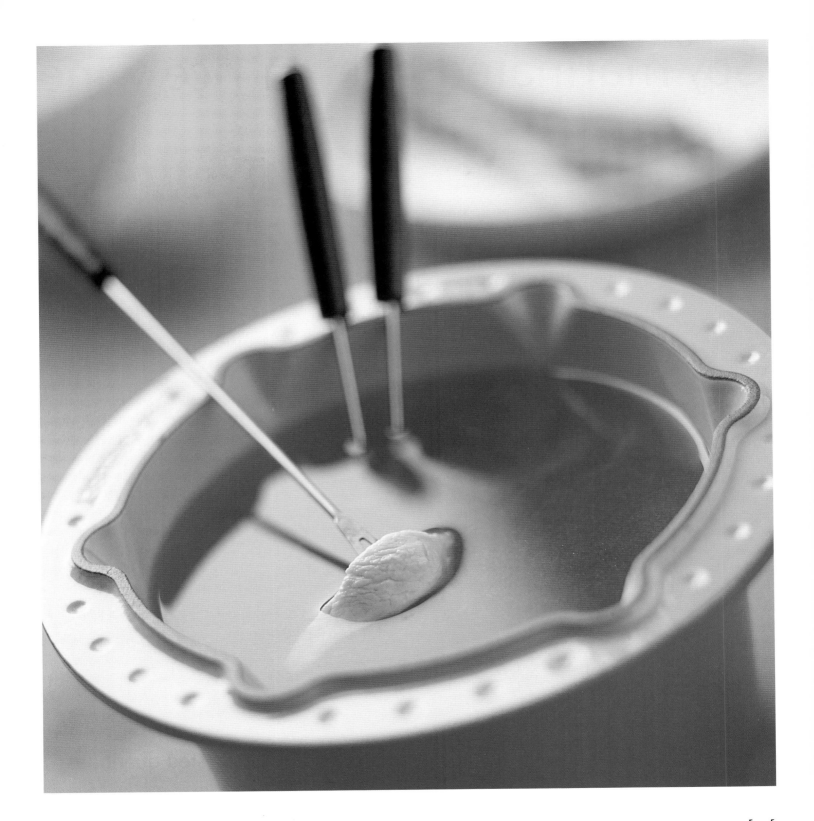

Soy-marinated beef in rice wine

3 lb (1.5 kg) beef flank (skirt) steak, trimmed

FOR MARINADE

1 teaspoon ground (powdered) ginger

1 teaspoon dry (powdered) mustard

1 tablespoons molasses or golden syrup

1/2 cup (4 fl oz/125 ml) soy sauce

1/4 cup (2 fl oz/60 ml) peanut oil

3 cloves garlic, finely chopped

vegetable crudités of choice

3–5 cups (24–40 fl oz/750 ml–1.25 L) rice wine or
  sake

Curried mayonnaise (see page 102) or other
  dipping sauces of choice

steamed rice, green salad and Asian pickles, for
  serving (optional)

Thinly slice beef, cutting across the grain. In a large, shallow bowl, stir together all the marinade ingredients and toss with the beef. Cover and refrigerate for at least 2 hours or overnight.

When ready to serve, drain meat and arrange it on a platter. Arrange vegetables on a separate platter.

Fill a stoneware or metal fondue pot two-thirds full with the wine. At the table, heat to a rapid simmer. Secure meat and vegetables onto skewers, letting the end of each skewer protrude by 1/2 inch (12 mm). Plunge each skewer into the pot and cook strips of meat 1–2 minutes, cubes 3–5 minutes. Cook vegetables 3–5 minutes, depending on the vegetable. Drain and dip into individual bowls of sauce. Accompany with bowls of steamed rice, green salad, and if desired, Asian pickles.

Serves 6

Note: This marinated meat is also excellent fried in a Burgundian fondue (see recipe pages 62–78).

Suggested quantities

1/2–1 cup cooked rice per person

SOY-MARINATED BEEF IN RICE WINE

Spicy crab and shrimp beer boil

FOR SEAFOOD PLATTER

5 lb (2.5 kg) cooked crab

2 1/2 lb (1.25 kg) jumbo shrimp (king prawns)

4 lb (2 kg) live crawfish (crayfish/yabbies)
  (optional)

FOR BEER BOIL

2 teaspoons mustard seed

1 teaspoon coarsely ground pepper

6 whole cloves

1 teaspoon ground mace (optional)

1 tablespoon paprika

1¹/₂ tablespoons dried thyme, crumbled

2 teaspoons cayenne pepper, or more to taste

1 tablespoon fennel seed

2 bay leaves, crumbled

¹/₄ cup rock salt

1 stalk celery, coarsely chopped or 2 teaspoons
  celery seed, ground

1-inch (2.5-cm) piece fresh ginger, thinly sliced

4–5 cups lager beer

seasoned salt and Drawn butter (see page 103),
  for dipping

sourdough bread and tossed green salad, for serving

Clean crab by pulling off the apron flap from under its shell. Pry off the top shell and rinse away the breathing ducts or lungs. Break or cut the body in half, or in larger crabs, cut into smaller pieces. Twist off claws. Arrange crab parts on a platter. If the shrimp still have their heads, twist them off and reserve to add to the beer boil for added flavor; do not shell. Rinse crawfish in a colander then place in the freezer for 30 minutes until dead. (This also prevents them from splashing hot liquid at the table.) Take care when handling the crawfish, as their pincers are sharp. Use tongs, or grab them directly behind the head.

To make the beer boil: In a mortar, combine all the dry seasonings, except salt; grind to a powder with a pestle.

Fill a stoneware or nonreactive metal fondue pot about half-full with beer and add dry seasonings, salt, ginger, and if using, chopped celery. At the table, bring to a rapid simmer. Add just enough of the crab to comfortably fit in the pot. Simmer until the flesh is hot, 3–5 minutes. Using a small wire-mesh skimmer. Add shrimp to the pot and cook until flesh is firm, about 3 minutes. Add the crawfish and cook until color changes and the flesh is firm, 3–5 minutes. Let guests shell their own shrimp and crawfish, and use fondue forks to extract the crabmeat from the shell.

Supply bibs, finger bowls, hand towels, and bowls for the shells. Accompany with small bowls of seasoned salt and drawn butter. Serve with sourdough bread and tossed green salad.

Serves 6

Note: A clean electric coffee grinder is excellent for grinding the dry seasonings for this recipe.

SPICY CRAB AND SHRIMP BEER BOIL

Seafood in court bouillon

1 lobster tail (optional)

1 lb (500 g) raw medium shrimp (prawns), shelled
(tails left on and shells reserved)

10-oz (300-g) jar fresh oysters

1 can (14 oz/440 g) abalone (optional)

12 oz (375 g) scallops or squid (calamari) rings

36 small clams, scrubbed

Drawn butter or Quick ponzu (see page 103),
for dipping

1½ lb (750 g) firm white fish fillets such as cod,
perch, or halibut, cut into bite-sized pieces

FOR COURT BOUILLON

5 cups (40 fl oz/1.25 L) water

reserved shrimp and lobster shells (above)

reserved oyster liqueur and abalone juice (above)

2 carrots, peeled and coarsely chopped

1 onion, diced

4 sprigs parsley

1 teaspoon dried thyme

2 bay leaves

½ teaspoon peppercorns

1 teaspoon salt

1 clove garlic, crushed

pinch of cayenne pepper

1½ cups (12 fl oz/375 ml) white wine

crusty bread, for serving

To prepare court bouillon: In a large nonreactive saucepan, combine all ingredients, cover and bring to a boil. Remove lid, reduce heat and simmer for 20 minutes. When ready to serve, strain and transfer to a fondue pot maintianing a gentle simmer, about 325–350°F (160–175°C). The liquid should fill two-thirds of the pot. If not, add boiling water. (Note: if flavoring court bouillon with seafood shells (see below), strain and discard shells before bringing liquid to the table.)

If using the lobster, use shears to cut up and along the under-ribs of the shell; pry open and remove the meat from its shell. Reserve the shells for the bouillon. "Butterfly" the shrimp by slicing deeply lengthwise along the back to remove the vein. Do not cut all the way through. Gently score the underside of shrimp to prevent curling. Drain oysters, reserving their liquor for the court bouillon.

If using, cut lobster meat into medallions. Drain the abalone, if using, adding its juice to the bouillon; slice paper-thin. Arrange all seafood attractively on a platter, cover, and refrigerate until required.

To serve, use small wire-mesh skimmers, skewers, or chopsticks to dip the seafood into the simmering broth. Cook shrimp about 3 minutes. The clams are done when open, 2–3 minutes; discard any that do not open. Cook white fish and lobster until white throughout, about 2 minutes. Cook scallops until just opaque, 1–2 minutes. The squid will take only 1 minute, and the oysters 30 seconds. Add the abalone at the end and cook about 30 seconds to just heat through. Take care not to overcook the seafood, or it will be tough. Remove from the broth and dip into sauces. At the end, serve cups of the simmering cooking liquid. Accompany with crusty bread, finger bowls and towels.

Serves 6

fondues

Fundamentally bourguignonne

3 lb (1.5 kg) veal loin or beef tenderloin (fillet), trimmed

parsley sprigs, for garnish

3–5 cups (24–40fl oz/750 ml–1.25 L) grapeseed or peanut oil, or Clarified butter (see page 105) or ghee, melted, or a combination

salt and freshly ground pepper to taste

Mounted béarnaise (see page 102) plus other dipping sauces of choice, for serving

salad, pickled onions, olives and bread, for serving

Cut meat into ¾-inch (2-cm) cubes and arrange on a platter. Garnish with parsley, cover and refrigerate. Meanwhile, fill a fondue pot no more than one-third with the oil, butter and/or ghee. At the table, heat to 325–350°F (165–175°C). Sprinkle the meat with salt and pepper. Secure a piece of meat onto a skewer, with the skewer protruding by ½ inch (12 mm), and cook until the desired doneness, 2–3 minutes.

Remove meat from the oil. Serve with the dipping sauces alongside. Accompany with a mushroom or green salad, pickled onions, olives, and bread. Wait until the oil, butter, or ghee has cooled completely before removing the pot from the table.

Serves 6

Variations

Substitute thin strips of beef flank (skirt) and thread them on the skewers. Cook for 1 minute. Game meat also works well here, especially venison loin. If desired, rub first with a spice rub (see recipe page 64) for added flavor.

Aromatic oil marinade (see page 104) adds flavor to any tender beef, veal, pork loin, and boneless chicken. Marinate the cubed or diced meat for several hours, then proceed as above.

Beef with a spice rub

FOR SPICE RUB

1 tablespoon juniper berries

1 tablespoon peppercorns

1 teaspoon whole allspice

$^1/_4$ teaspoon ground (powdered) ginger

$^1/_2$ teaspoon dry (powdered) mustard

2 bay leaves, crumbled

$^1/_4$ cup (2 oz/60 g) coarse salt

3 lb (1.5 kg) beef flank (skirt) steak, trimmed

parsley sprigs, for garnish

3–5 cups (24–40 fl oz/750 ml–1.25 L) grapeseed or
   peanut oil

Mounted béarnaise (see page 102) or other
   dipping sauces of choice, for serving

To make the rub: In a mortar, combine all the rub ingredients except the bay leaves and salt. Grind to a coarse powder. Stir in bay leaves and salt. Pat rub all over the beef. Cover and refrigerate for 2–3 hours.

When ready to serve, scrape off the seasoning and thinly slice meat across the grain. Arrange slices on a serving platter and garnish with parsley. Pour oil into a metal fondue pot, filling it no more than one-third full. At the table, heat to 325–350°F (165–175°C). Thread the meat on skewers, letting them protrude by $^1/_2$ inch (12 mm). Cook meat until the desired doneness, about 1 minute. Remove from the pot and dip directly into individual bowls of sauce. Let oil cool fully before removing the pot from the table.

Serves 6

BEEF WITH A SPICE RUB

Vegetable and corn fondue

1 lb (500 g) small new potatoes (chats), scrubbed

1 sweet potato, peeled

2 carrots, peeled

1 parsnip, peeled

1 lb (500 g) winter squash or pumpkin, peeled and
   seeded

1 rutabaga (Swede), peeled

1 celeriac (celery root), peeled (optional)

$^1\!/_2$ cup (4 fl oz/125 ml) apple cider vinegar

2 fresh ears corn, shucked

3–5 cups ($1^1\!/_2$–$2^1\!/_2$ lb/750 g–1.25 kg) clarified
   butter or ghee, melted

salt and freshly ground pepper to taste

Mounted béarnaise, (see page 102) Anchovy sauce
   (see page 103), or other dipping sauces, for
   serving

In a large pot of salted water, boil potatoes until barely tender when skewered, about 10 minutes. Drain and let cool. Cut sweet potato, carrots, parsnip, squash or pumpkin, rutabaga, and celeriac into 1-inch (2.5-cm) cubes. Plunge into a large pot of salted boiling water and add vinegar. Cook for exactly 3 minutes after the water returns to a boil and then drain. Lay the vegetables out on a large baking sheet to cool, allowing the steam to evaporate fully. Cut corn into 1-inch-thick (2.5-cm) rounds, then cut in half to make moons. (The corn does not require precooking.)

Fill a metal fondue pot, no more than one-third full with clarified butter or ghee. At the table, heat to 325–350°F (165–175°C). Secure a piece of vegetable onto a skewer, letting the skewer protrude by $^1\!/_2$ inch (12 mm). Cook until desired doneness, 3–5 minutes. Remove from the oil. Sprinkle with salt and pepper. Serve with dipping sauces alongside. Let butter or ghee cool completely before removing the pot from the table.

Serves 6

Greek lamb fondue

3 lb (1.5 kg) lamb loin or boneless leg, trimmed
and cut into $^{3}/_{4}$-inch (2-cm) cubes

$^{1}/_{4}$ cup (2 fl oz/60 ml) fresh lemon juice

$^{1}/_{3}$ cup (3 fl oz/90 ml) olive oil

2 teaspoons dried oregano

1 teaspoon dried finely chopped garlic

1 teaspoon salt

oregano, for garnish (optional)

3–5 cups (24–40 fl oz/750 ml–1.25 L) grapeseed or
peanut oil or Clarified butter (see page 105) or
ghee, melted or a combination

4 unpeeled cloves garlic

slices of crusty (or toasted) bread, mint jelly,
Mounted béarnaise (see page 102), Anchovy
sauce (see page 103) and other sauces, for
serving

Toss lamb with lemon juice, olive oil, oregano, and garlic. Cover and refrigerate for 2–3 hours. Toss in salt and arrange on a serving platter. If desired, garnish with fresh oregano.

Fill a metal fondue pot one-third full with oil, clarified butter, ghee, or a combination; do not overfill. At the table, heat to 325–350°F (165–175°C). Toss garlic cloves and the fresh oregano, if using, into the pot to flavor the oil. Remove with a small wire-mesh skimmer when they turn brown. Discard oregano but spread garlic on the bread. Insert skewers into the lamb cubes, letting the skewer protrude by $^{1}/_{2}$ inch (12 mm), and plunge them into the pot and cook until the desired doneness, 2–3 minutes. Serve with dipping sauces alongside. Let oil, butter, or ghee cool completely before removing the pot from the table.

Serves 6

Variation

Bread: 1 loaf per 2–3 persons, or about twenty 1-inch (2.5-cm) cubes per person

GREEK LAMB FONDUE

Garlic shrimp

36 raw jumbo shrimp (king prawns), about 2 lb (1 kg), shelled and deveined (tails left on)

1 whole bulb garlic

1 teaspoon red chili pepper flakes

$1/3$ cup (3 fl oz/90 ml) olive oil

$1/4$ cup (2 fl oz/60 ml) dry white wine

1 teaspoon salt

3–5 cups (1 $1/2$–2 $1/2$ lb/750 g–1.25 kg) Clarified butter (see page 105) or ghee

Quick ponzu (see page 103) plus other dipping sauces of choice

slices of crusty or toasted bread, for serving

Carefully score the underside of each shrimp with 2 or 3 shallow slashes to prevent curling.

Separate cloves from the garlic bulb and peel half of them; finely chop. Reserve unpeeled cloves to flavor the oil.

In a medium bowl, combine chopped garlic, pepper flakes, oil, wine, and salt. Add shrimp and toss to coat. Cover and refrigerate for 2–3 hours. When ready to serve, drain the shrimp. Arrange them on a platter and bring to the table.

Fill a metal fondue pot no more than one-third full with clarified butter or ghee and add unpeeled garlic. At the table, heat to 325–350°F (165–175°C). Skewer a shrimp through each end, letting skewer protrude by $1/2$ inch (12 mm). Plunge shrimp into the hot oil and cook until evenly pink, about 2 minutes. Remove from oil and drain. Serve with dipping sauces. After the initial 20 minutes garlic cloves will become lightly golden. When garlic cloves soften, remove them from the oil and press onto bread slices. Let butter or ghee cool completely before removing the pot from the table.

Serves 4–6

Variation

Garlic calamari: If using whole squid, pull tentacles and head from the body, and cut away from just in front of the eyes. Use your fingers to scoop out the innards and inner spearlike cartilage from the tube. Rinse well. Keep tentacles whole. Frozen squid tubes work equally well; thaw and cut into $1/2$-inch-wide (12-mm) rings. Proceed as in the master recipe, cooking 1 minute.

GARLIC SHRIMP

Ham and sesame cubes

1 cup (4 oz/125 g) sesame seeds, lightly toasted

3 lb (1.5 kg) ham, cut into ³/₄-inch (2-cm) cubes

3 tablespoons soy sauce

3–5 cups (24–40 fl oz/750 ml–1.25 L) grapeseed or
   peanut oil, or Clarified butter (see page 105) or
   ghee, melted or a combination

Quick Chinese mustard (see page 104)

ketchup (tomato sauce), chutney, soy sauce
   and/or horseradish, for serving

To toast sesame seeds: Preheat oven to 375°F (190°C/Gas 5). Pour seeds onto a rimmed baking sheet and toast in the oven until lightly golden, 7–10 minutes. Shake occasionally to ensure even browning.

Toss ham with the soy sauce and arrange on a platter; sprinkle with 1 tablespoon sesame seeds. Fill a metal fondue pot no more than one-third full with oil, clarified butter, or ghee, or a combination. At the table, heat to 325–350°F (165–175°C). Pierce a cube of ham with a skewer. Plunge ham into the hot oil and cook for about 2 minutes. Drain. Dip into the mustard or one of the condiments, then into the remaining sesame seeds. Let oil, butter, or ghee cool completely before removing the pot from the table.

Serves 4–6

HAM AND SESAME CUBES

Deviled kidneys and chicken livers

2 lb (1 kg) lamb or calf kidneys

2 tablespoons plus 1 teaspoon salt

4 cups (32 fl oz/1 L) ice water

3 tablespoons fresh lemon juice

Quick Chinese mustard (see page 104)

1 tablespoon chopped fresh parsley

1 teaspoon coarsely ground pepper

3–5 cups (1½–2½ lb/750 g–1.25 kg) Clarified
  butter (see page 105) or ghee, melted

boiled rice and salad, for serving

Trim kidneys of all visible fat. Slice in half lengthwise, then use kitchen shears to cut away the white core. Pull away any membrane. Cut calf kidneys into ¾-inch (2-cm) pieces; cut lamb kidneys in half crosswise, creating 2 fat crescents.

Dissolve 2 tablespoons salt in the water and add 2 tablespoons lemon juice. Add kidneys and let soak for 15 minutes. Drain and pat dry with paper towels. Put kidney pieces in a medium bowl and add 2 tablespoons of mustard, parsley, and remaining 1 tablespoon lemon juice and 1 teaspoon salt; toss to coat evenly. Pierce the pieces onto skewers. Arrange skewers on a serving plate and sprinkle with pepper. Cover and refrigerate until ready.

Fill a metal fondue pot no more than one-third full with clarified butter or ghee. At the table, heat to 325–350°F (165–175°C). Plunge skewers into butter and cook for about 3 minutes. Serve with additional mustard, boiled rice, and a side salad. Let butter or ghee cool completely before removing the pot from the table.

Serves 4–6

Variation

Deviled chicken livers: Substitute trimmed chicken livers for the kidneys, but do not soak in water. Proceed as above, cooking for 1–2 minutes. If desired, add pitted prunes and dates or water chestnuts to the skewers.

Curried fish strips

2 lb (1 kg) firm white fish fillets, such as cod, flounder or halibut

1 cup (5 oz/150 g) all-purpose (plain) flour

1/2 teaspoon cayenne pepper

2 tablespoons curry powder

1 teaspoon salt

3–6 eggs

3–5 cups (24–40 fl oz/750 ml–1.25 L) grapeseed or peanut oil, or Clarified butter (see page 105) or ghee, melted or a combination

Mounted béarnaise (see page 102), Curried mayonnaise (see page 102), bottled tartare sauce and/or soy sauce, for dipping

Cut fish into strips 2 inches (5 cm) long, 1 inch (2.5 cm) wide, and 1/2 inch (12 mm) thick. Thread these onto skewers, letting the end of each skewer protrude by 1/2 inch (12 mm).

Sift flour, cayenne, curry powder, and salt together into a shallow bowl. Dredge fish in the seasoned flour. Place on a tray, with waxed paper between the layers, and refrigerate up to 6 hours, or until ready to serve.

To serve, arrange fish on a serving platter. Place 1 egg in each of 6 small, deep bowls, or use 3 bowls to be shared between 2 people. Lightly beat eggs. Fill a metal fondue pot one-third full with oil, butter, or ghee. At the table, heat to 325–350°F (165–175°C). Dip skewers in the egg, drain, and plunge into the hot oil. (Note: If the bowls are too shallow, use a pastry brush to coat skewers with egg dip.) Fry until lightly golden, about 2 minutes. If fish pieces overcook and break during cooking, use a small wire-mesh skimmer or slotted spoon to retrieve them. Serve with dipping sauces alongside. Let oil, butter, or ghee cool completely before removing the pot from the table.

Serves 6

CURRIED FISH STRIPS

Vinegar-dipped potatoes

2 lb (1 kg) unpeeled small new potatoes (chats),
   well scrubbed

1 1/2 cups (12 fl oz/375 ml) apple cider vinegar

1 cup (8 fl oz/250 ml) peanut or olive oil

1/2 cup (4 oz/125 g) butter

1 large onion, finely chopped

2 teaspoons whole caraway or cumin seed

2 teaspoons salt

1/2 teaspoon ground pepper

mustard, horseradish, Anchovy sauce (see page
   103), Curried mayonnaise (see page 102), or
   sauces of choice

Cook potatoes in a large pot of salted boiling water until barely tender when skewered, 8–10 minutes. Drain.

Meanwhile, combine all remaining ingredients, except the sauce, in a medium saucepan. Bring to a boil, reduce heat, and simmer for 5 minutes. Transfer to a warmed nonreactive fondue pot and add potatoes. At the table, simmer potatoes until tender but not overcooked, about 20 minutes. Prick potato to determine doneness. (Note: Unlike other Burgundian fondues, the potatoes are not fried; the large quantity of vinegar flavoring the oil prevents that.) Skewer potatoes with fondue forks, and dip into individual bowls of sauce.

Serves 6

Shabu shabu

3 lb (1.5 kg) well-marbled beef tenderloin (fillet)
   or sirloin

1 lb (500 g) soft tofu, cut into $3/_4$–1 inch
   (2–2.5 cm) cubes, rinsed

1 bunch scallions (shallots/spring onions), cut
   into 2-inch-diagonal (5-cm) pieces

leaves from $1/_4$ head Chinese napa cabbage

2 carrots, peeled and cut into thin rounds

1 bunch spinach or chrysanthemum leaves,
   stemmed

8-inch (20-cm) piece konbu

Quick ponzu (see page 103), for dipping

steamed rice, for serving

Cut meat wafer-thin across the grain. Arrange slices attractively, slightly overlapping, on a platter or individual plates. Cover and refrigerate until needed.

Soak tofu in fresh water for 20 minutes; drain. Decoratively arrange tofu and vegetables on a platter.

Wipe konbu with a damp cloth to remove any grit. Place konbu in a Japanese donabe or fondue pot (if using a coal firepot, see pages 14–15 for instructions). Fill two-thirds full with cold water. At the table, bring to a rapid simmer and remove kelp. Maintain liquid at a rapid simmer.

To cook meat and vegetables: Use chopsticks or fondue forks to "swish" pieces of meat in the stock to the desired doneness, about 10 seconds. Dip into the ponzu. Place vegetable pieces in the broth until the desired doneness, 2–5 minutes. Retrieve vegetables using small wire-mesh skimmers. Accompany with bowls of steamed rice.

Serves 6

Chicken mizutaki

3 lb (1.5 kg) boneless, skinless chicken thighs and
  breasts, cut into bite-sized pieces

20 dried black (shiitake) mushrooms

1/2 bunch scallions (shallots/spring onions)

1 bunch asparagus, trimmed

1 green bell pepper (capsicum), seeded

leaves from 1/4 head Chinese napa cabbage

2 carrots, peeled and cut into thin rounds

1/4 cauliflower, broken into small florets, stems
  peeled and sliced

1 head broccoli, broken into small florets, stems
  peeled and sliced

4–6 cups (32–48 fl oz/1–1.5 L) Chicken broth (see
  page 105)

Mizutaki sauce (see page 104) or Quick ponzu (see
  page 103), for dipping

steamed rice, for serving

Put chicken pieces in a sieve. Pour boiling water over them and drain. Let cool. Arrange pieces on a serving platter. Cover and refrigerate until ready to serve.

Soak mushrooms in warm water for 20 minutes, or until soft. Drain. Use scissors to snip off the tough stems; discard. Cut scallions and asparagus into 2-inch (5-cm) lengths. Cut the bell pepper into 2-inch-long sticks. Arrange vegetables in groups attractively on a platter and cover; refrigerate until ready to serve.

To serve, pour broth into a Japanese donabe or a fondue pot, filling it about two-thirds full. (If using a coal firepot, refer to pages 14–15 for instructions.) At the table, bring to a rapid simmer. Add vegetables as desired, retrieving loose vegetable pieces with a small wire-mesh skimmer. Use chopsticks to dip pieces of chicken in the broth and cook until done, no less than 3 minutes. Accompany with dipping sauces and eat with bowls of steamed rice. When finished, ladle the broth into the rice bowls.

Serves 6

Hints

Both Shabu shabu and Chicken mizutaki are nabemono, Japanese one-pot dishes cooked at the table. The dipping sauces served with them may be garnished with salt, sesame seeds, and a pinch of cayenne or sansho (Japanese pepper). Accompany with assorted tart pickled vegetables, particularly Japanese tsukemono.

CHICKEN MIZUTAKI

Korean hot pot

FOR MARINADE

2 tablespoons sesame seeds, lightly toasted (see page 72)

$1/2$ cup (4 fl oz/125 ml) soy sauce

2 tablespoons rice vinegar or distilled white vinegar

3 tablespoons peanut oil, preferably cold-pressed

1 clove garlic, crushed

FOR MEATS

$1^1/2$ lb (750 g) boneless beef shank (leg shin), trimmed

1 lb (500 g) ground (minced) pork

2 tablespoons pine nuts

$1/2$ cup (2 oz/60 g) cornstarch (cornflour)

2 eggs, lightly beaten

2–4 tablespoons peanut oil or any good-quality oil

FOR VEGETABLES

10 oz (300 g) button mushrooms

1 daikon (Japanese white radish) or 2 turnips, peeled

3 carrots, peeled

2 stalks celery

leaves from $1/4$ head Chinese napa cabbage, quartered

$1/2$ bunch scallions (shallots/spring onions), cut into 2-inch (5-cm) pieces

6 hard-cooked eggs, shelled

4 cups (32 fl oz/1 L) Enriched meat stock (see page 105)

steamed rice, Korean vinegar dipping sauce (see page 105) and kimchi, for serving

In a mortar, lightly crush sesame seeds with a pestle. Stir in remaining marinade ingredients. Measure out $1/4$ cup (2 fl oz/60 ml) marinade and reserve for pork. Slice beef as thinly as possible, then cut into matchsticks (thin cuts are important, as this beef is chewy). Toss slices in marinade and set aside.

Use your hands to blend the reserved marinade into the ground pork. Knead for several minutes, as this helps to create a firm texture that will not break up during cooking. Pinch off a small ball and place a pine nut in its center. Using hands to prevent sticking, form into a ball. Continue until all meat and nuts are used up. You should have about 50 meatballs. Place meatballs on a rimmed baking sheet and sieve the cornstarch over; shake the tray to coat the meatballs. Brush off any excess cornstarch. Dip each meatball into the beaten egg. In a skillet over medium heat, heat oil and brown the meat on all sides until cooked through, about 5 minutes. Set aside. You may need to do this in 2 batches; if so, use additional oil.

To prepare vegetables: Wipe mushrooms with a damp cloth to remove grit. If mushrooms are large, slice in half. Cut daikon or turnips into $1/8$-inch-thick (3-mm) strips about 2 inches (5 cm) long; do the same with the carrots. Cut celery stalks into 2-inch-long (5-cm) pieces, then slice pieces into thin sticks.

Arrange vegetables, meats, and whole eggs by group, attractively in a firepot or metal fondue pot. (If using a coal firepot, see page 14–15 for instructions.) Fill pot with enough broth to the rim, but do not overfill.

At the table, bring to a rapid simmer. (Alternatively, bring the broth to a boil on the stove and pour into the pot.) Cook to the desired doneness, about 5 minutes. Use small wire-mesh skimmers and chopsticks to transfer food from the pot to individual bowls of steamed rice. Accompany with dipping sauce and kimchi.

Serves 6

Coconut and seafood hot pot

FOR BROTH

1 tablespoon peanut oil or any good-quality oil

6 shallots (French shallots), coarsely chopped

2 cloves garlic, crushed

1/2-inch (12-mm) piece galangal or fresh ginger, thinly sliced

1 teaspoon red pepper flakes

1 tablespoon salt

2 teaspoons sugar

4 cups (32 fl oz/1 L) water, or more as needed

1 1/2 cups (12 fl oz/375 ml) thin coconut cream or coconut milk

2 stalks lemongrass, white part only

juice from 3 limes

FOR SEAFOOD PLATTER

2 lb (1 kg) jumbo shrimp (king prawns)

3/4 lb (375 g) scallops or squid (calamari) rings

10 oz (300 g) jar oysters

1 1/2 lb (750 g) firm white fish fillets, such as cod, snapper or halibut

FOR VEGETABLE PLATTER

1 telegraph or long cucumber, peeled, halved lengthwise, and seeded

1 bunch green onions, cut into 2-inch (5-cm) lengths

8 oz (250 g) green beans, cut into 2-inch (5-cm) lengths

4 oz (125 g) bean sprouts

1 bunch fresh cilantro (fresh coriander), coarsely chopped

Drawn butter (see page 103) and Nuoc cham sauce (see page 103), for dipping

In a large saucepan set over medium-high heat, heat oil and sauté shallots and garlic until golden, 2–3 minutes. Add all remaining broth ingredients except the lime juice. Bring to a rapid simmer. Transfer to the firepot or a stoneware or metal fondue pot, filling it two-thirds full. If necessary, add boiling water. (If using a coal firepot, see pages 14–15 for instructions.)

To prepare seafood platter: Remove shrimp heads and shells. Keep tails intact. If using raw shrimp, "Butterfly" shrimp by slicing deeply lengthwise along the back to remove the vein. Do not cut all the way through. Gently score the underside of the shrimp to prevent curling. If scallops still have their roe, retain, but cut away the black vein around the scallop. Drain the oysters, adding their liquid to the court bouillon. Remove all skin and bones from the fish fillets and cut into bite-sized pieces. Arrange seafood attractively on a platter, cover and refrigerate until required.

To prepare the vegetable platter: Cut cucumber in thin semi-circles. Arrange all vegetables on a platter and sprinkle generously with the cilantro. Cover and refrigerate until ready to serve.

When ready to serve, add lime juice to the pot, and if using, the reserved coconut water. Drop individual pieces of vegetable into the simmering broth and cook until desired doneness, about 2 minutes for the cucumber, bean sprouts and scallions, and up to 5 minutes for the beans. Use small wire-mesh skimmers or skewers to secure each piece of shellfish and cook till just done. Precooked seafood merely requires heating through, while raw shellfish a few minutes: 3 minutes for shrimp, 1–2 minutes for scallops and 1 minute for squid. Do not overcook seafood. Remove from the broth and eat as is or dipped into Drawn butter or Quick ponzu.

Spoon broth into individual soup bowls (note: the ginger and lemongrass are not eaten) and if desired, season with Nuoc cham sauce or plain fish sauce.

Serves 6

COCONUT AND SEAFOOD HOT POT

Vietnamese lau

2 packets (40 sheets) round rice paper

FOR BEEF PLATTER

1 medium onion, thinly sliced

1 tablespoon rice vinegar or distilled white vinegar

3 lb (1.5 kg) eye of beef round, sirloin, or tenderloin (fillet), trimmed and cut into paper-thin slices

2 tablespoons Asian sesame oil

2 teaspoons coarsely ground pepper

FOR VEGETABLE PLATTER

leaves from 3 heads butter (Boston) lettuce

1 telegraph or long cucumber, peeled, halved lengthwise and seeded

1 bunch scallions (shallots/spring onions), cut into 2-inch (5-cm) lengths

4 oz (125 g) bean sprouts

sprigs from 1 bunch fresh mint

1 bunch fresh cilantro (fresh coriander)

1 bunch Thai or sweet basil

FOR BROTH

2 tablespoons peanut oil or any good quality oil

2 garlic cloves, thinly sliced

1-inch (2.5-cm) piece fresh ginger, thinly sliced

1 stalk lemongrass, white part only, cut into thin rounds (optional)

1 cup (8 fl oz/250 ml) rice vinegar or distilled white vinegar

5 cups (40 fl oz/1.25 L) water

1 tablespoon salt

3 tablespoons sugar

1 cup (5 oz/150 g) peanuts (ground nuts), crushed, for serving and Nuoc cham sauce (see page 103), for dipping

Cover rice paper with a damp cloth and wrap tightly with plastic wrap until needed. About 1 hour before the meal, dip each rice paper in warm water for 10 seconds to soften. Stack, interspersing each rice paper with well-moistened waxed paper, and wrap stack in plastic wrap to prevent drying. Should they stick together, brush liberally with water at the table.

To prepare beef platter: In a small bowl, toss onion slices with vinegar. Arrange beef attractively on 2 platters, overlapping as little as possible. Drizzle with oil and sprinkle with pepper. Drain onions, discarding vinegar, and break onion slices into rings. Place decoratively over meat. Cover and refrigerate until ready to serve.

To prepare vegetable platter: Tear any large lettuce leaves in half. Cut away the stiff cores, as these are prone to tear the rice paper when rolled. Cut cucumber into very thin semi-circles. Arrange all vegetables in groups and serve on a platter. Cover and refrigerate until ready to serve.

To make broth: In a large saucepan, heat oil over medium heat. Add garlic and ginger and sauté until fragrant, 1–2 minutes. Do not let the garlic brown. Add remaining broth ingredients and bring to a rapid simmer. Strain broth into a hot pot or metal fondue pot on the table. (If using a coal firepot, see pages 14–15 for instructions.) (The broth should fill the pot about two-thirds full; if not, add boiling water to the desired depth.) At the table, bring to a rapid simmer.

To serve, lay a sheet of softened rice paper on a plate and center a lettuce leaf, a few herb sprigs, and some marinated onions from the meat platter. Drop a piece of meat into the simmering liquid until the desired doneness, about 10 seconds. Retrieve with chopsticks or a wire-mesh skimmer. Lay meat over vegetables. If desired, sprinkle with ground peanuts, then fold to enclose the bottom and top. Roll up. (If papers tear, fold sheets in half to a double thickness, and roll, leaving the two ends exposed.) The finished roll should be the size of a thick cigar. Dip in Nuoc cham sauce and eat with your fingers.

Serves 6

VIETNAMESE LAU

Mongolian firepot

FOR MEAT PLATTERS

12 oz (375 g) flank steak (skirt steak)

12 oz (375 g) boneless lean lamb, such as loin

4 boneless, skinless chicken breast halves, thinly sliced

2 tablespoons soy sauce

2 tablespoons Asian sesame oil

$1/2$-inch (12-mm) piece fresh ginger, grated

1 small clove garlic, crushed

FOR VEGETABLE PLATTERS

1 lb (500 g) soft tofu, cut into $3/4$-inch (2-cm) cubes

2 turnips or 1 rutabaga (Swede), peeled

leaves from $1/4$ head Chinese napa cabbage

$1/2$ bunch spinach, stemmed

4 oz (125 g) mushrooms

4 oz (125 g) snow peas (mange-tout), trimmed

1 bunch scallions (shallots/spring onions), cut into 2-inch
  (5-cm) lengths

4–6 cups (32–48 fl oz/1–1.5 L) Enriched meat stock (see page 105)

2 tablespoons rice wine or dry sherry

Mongolian firepot dip (see page 104)

condiments of choice, such as plum sauce, hoisin sauce,
  and satay sauce

6 eggs (optional)

4 oz (125 g) cellophane (bean thread) noodles

Cut beef and lamb into paper-thin slices and lay them slightly overlapping on platters or individual plates. In a medium bowl, combine soy sauce, sesame oil, ginger, and garlic. Add the chicken and toss to coat. Arrange chicken on a separate platter. Wrap and refrigerate the meat and chicken until ready to use.

Meanwhile, prepare the vegetable platter: Soak tofu in water for 20 minutes, then drain. Halve any large mushrooms. Cut turnips or rutabaga into thin strips about 2 inches (5 cm) long. Arrange all the vegetables decoratively on a serving platter or plates.

Prepare coals for a firepot, if using (see pages 14–15 for instructions). Add stock and wine to a firepot or a metal fondue pot. Bring to a rapid simmer. At the table, have guests individually cook their meats and vegetables to desired doneness, using small wire ladles, chopsticks, or skewers. Meats will cook between 10 to no more than 20 seconds, depending on thickness and desired doneness. Spinach cooks within 10 seconds, but other vegetables may take 2 minutes or longer. Serve the dipping sauce and condiments alongside. If desired, break an egg into individual small bowls, beat lightly, and serve as a second dipping sauce. Serve individual bowls of steamed rice alongside, adding a little of the cooking broth to the rice.

Midway through the meal, soak the noodles in hot water for 10 minutes; drain and set aside. When guests have finished the meat and vegetables, add the noodles to the cooking broth. Ladle bowls of broth and noodles for each diner.

Serves 6

fondues

Classic chocolate fondue

$^1/_2$ cup (4 fl oz/125 ml) cream

2 tablespoons kirsch, triple sec, or brandy

9 oz (280 g) milk chocolate, preferably Swiss, chopped

fruits including: dried pineapple, mango and apple; fresh pears; fresh strawberries; fresh tangerine or mandarin slices

ladyfingers and profiteroles

In a double boiler over simmering water, heat the cream and liqueur or brandy. Add chocolate all at once, stirring until smooth. Transfer to a warmed stoneware or metal fondue pot and accompany with the fruits and sweets. Spear a piece of fruit with a fondue fork and dip the ladyfingers or profiteroles into the pot by hand.

Serves 6

Suggested quantities

Fruits, dried and fresh: about 2-4 oz (60-125 g) per person

Cookies (biscuits): about 4 per person

Hint

The original chocolate fondue was created in New York by a publicist for Toblerone chocolate. If desired, substitute Toblerone milk chocolate. Its bits of slightly melted honey and almond nougat enhance the flavor.

CLASSIC CHOCOLATE FONDUE

Gingered dark chocolate fondue

12 oz (375 g) jar candied ginger in syrup (see note)

¼ cup evaporated milk

1–2 tablespoons rum

6 oz (180 g) semisweet (plain) chocolate, chopped

fruits including: crystallized ginger pieces,
candied (glacéed) and fresh cherries, dried
pineapple, mango, and papaya, glazed apricots,
cut into thick strips, dates, hulled strawberries,
and pear slices

Drain ginger and reserve the liquid. (If it has totally crystallized, place it in a pan of warm water over low heat until melted, or in a microwave for 10 seconds.) Reserve the ginger pieces for later.

In a double boiler over simmering water, combine ginger syrup, milk, rum, and chocolate. Stir until melted. Transfer to a warmed stoneware or metal fondue pot. Skewer pieces of ginger or fruit on fondue forks and dip in the chocolate sauce. Remove and eat.

Serves 6

Note: Candied ginger in syrup is available at Asian supermarkets, often in decorative pottery jars. If unavailable, use crystallized ginger and add ½ teaspoon ground (powdered) ginger to the chocolate.

Suggested quantities

Fruits, dried and fresh: about 2-4 oz (60-125 g) per person

Cookies (biscuits): about 4 per person

GINGERED DARK CHOCOLATE FONDUE

Rocky road fondue

9 oz (280 g) milk chocolate, chopped

¹/₂ cup (4 fl oz/125 ml) sweetened condensed milk

¹/₂ cup (4 fl oz/125 ml) cream

1 tablespoon strong brewed coffee

1 tablespoon rum (optional)

8 oz (250 g) large marshmallows

¹/₂ cup (2¹/₂ oz/75 g) unsalted mixed nuts, lightly
  toasted and finely ground

pitted dates, ladyfingers, and cookies (biscuits),
  for serving

In a double boiler over simmering water, combine chocolate, milk, cream, coffee, and rum (if using). Stir until melted. Transfer to a warm fondue pot. Cut half the marshmallow quantity in half, rerserving the remaining whole marshmallows for the serving platter. At the table, briefly stir the cut marshmallows and all of the nuts into the melted chocolate. Serve the remaining marshmallows on a platter, along with the dates and cookies. Skewer them on fondue forks and dip into the chocolate sauce.

Serves 6

Note: To toast nuts, preheat oven to 375°F (190°C/Gas 5). Spread nuts on a rimmed baking sheet and bake until lightly browned, 8–12 minutes.

Suggested quantities

Fruits, dried and fresh: about 2-4 oz (60-125 g) per person

Cookies (biscuits): about 4 per person

ROCKY ROAD FONDUE

White chocolate and coconut fondue

¹/₂ cup (4 fl oz/125 ml) sweetened condensed milk

2 tablespoons triple sec

¹/₂ cup (4 fl oz/125 ml) thick coconut cream

8 oz (250 g) white chocolate, chopped

pinch of ground cinnamon

1 tablespoon flaked dried (desiccated) coconut

tropical fruits such as fresh pineapple, mango,
   papaya (paw paw), cut into bite-sized chunks,
   fresh strawberries, lichees and other tropical
   fruit

cookies (biscuits) such as coconut macaroons

In a double boiler over simmering water, heat milk, liqueur, and coconut cream. Add chocolate all at once, stirring until melted. Transfer to a warmed stoneware or metal fondue pot and sprinkle with the cinnamon and dried coconut. Dip macaroons by hand and skewer fruit with a fondue fork and immerse in the pot.

Serves 6

Suggested quantities

Fruits, dried and fresh: about 2-4 oz (60-125 g) per person

Cookies (biscuits): about 4 per person

Butterscotch fondue

4 tablespoons (2 oz/60 g) unsalted butter

²/₃ cup (5 fl oz/160 ml) light corn syrup

1¹/₄ cups (9 oz/280 g) firmly packed light brown
   sugar

²/₃ cup (5 fl oz/160 ml) cream

1 teaspoon vanilla extract (essence)

fruits and cookies (biscuits) of choice

In a medium saucepan, melt butter over medium heat. Add corn syrup and brown sugar, stirring until just dissolved. Bring to a boil and cook for 2–3 minutes. Remove from stove, then slowly stir in the cream and vanilla. Transfer to a warm fondue pot, and serve with fruit and cookies.

Serves 6

Suggested quantities

Fruits, dried and fresh: about 2-4 oz (60-125 g) per person

Cookies (biscuits): about 4 per person

sauces

Mounted béarnaise

4 tablespoons (2 fl oz/60 ml) dry white wine

3 eggs, separated

3 tablespoons tarragon vinegar

2 shallots (French shallots), very finely chopped

2 teaspoons chopped fresh tarragon, or 1 teaspoon dried tarragon

1/2 teaspoon coarsely ground pepper

1/2 teaspoon salt

3/4 cup (6 oz/185 g) Clarified butter (see page 105), melted and cooled to room temperature

1 tablespoon chopped fresh parsley

1 teaspoon chopped fresh chervil (optional)

In a small bowl, beat 2 tablespoons of wine into the egg yolks and set aside. In a large bowl, beat egg whites until stiff, glossy peaks form; set aside.

In a small saucepan, combine remaining 2 tablespoons wine, vinegar, shallots, tarragon, and pepper. Boil until reduced to a glaze, about 5 minutes. Let cool.

Whisk in the egg yolks and salt. Set the saucepan in a skillet of barely simmering water. Whisk constantly until mixture is thick and creamy. Remove from heat and very gradually whisk in the melted butter, returning pan to the simmering water periodically to keep the sauce warm. Gently fold in the beaten egg whites, parsley, and if using, chervil. Serve warm.

Makes about 2 cups (16 fl oz/500 ml)

Curried mayonnaise

2 eggs at room temperature

1 tablespoon fresh lemon juice

1 teaspoon salt

1/4 teaspoon finely ground white pepper

1 cup (8 fl oz/250 ml) peanut oil

1/2 cup (4 fl oz/125 ml) olive oil

1 tablespoon curry powder

1 teaspoon dijon mustard

In a food processor, combine 1 whole egg and 1 egg yolk (reserve remaining egg white for another use), lemon juice, salt, and pepper. Process for 5 seconds. With the machine running, very gradually drizzle in the oil in a very thin stream to make a thick sauce. Add curry powder and mustard and process until very thick.

Makes about 1½ cups (12 fl oz/375 ml)

Variation: A quick version may be made by stirring 1 tablespoon curry powder into 1 cup (8 fl oz/250 ml) commercial mayonnaise.

Tip: If the mayonnaise separates, pour mixture into a small jug. Thoroughly wash the blender or food processor container. Add 1 whole egg and process for a few seconds. With the machine running, very gradually add the separated mixture. The mayonnaise should rebind.

Anchovy sauce

2-oz (60-g) can anchovy fillets,
    drained
$^1/_4$ cup (2 fl oz/60 ml) milk
4 tablespoons (2 oz/60 g) butter
$^1/_2$ cup (4 fl oz/125 ml) olive oil
2 garlic cloves, very finely chopped
$^1/_4$ teaspoon coarsely ground pepper
$^1/_2$ cup ($^3/_4$ oz/20 g) chopped fresh
    parsley
salt to taste

In a small bowl, soak anchovy fillets in milk for about 15 minutes. Drain and discard the milk. Finely chop the anchovies.

In a small saucepan, melt butter with the oil over medium heat. Add garlic and sauté until fragrant, about 2 minutes; do not brown. Reduce heat to medium low. Add anchovies and pepper and cook for 15 minutes. Stir in the parsley and salt. Serve warm.

Makes about $^3/_4$ cup (6 fl oz/180 ml)

Drawn butter

$^1/_2$ cup (4 oz/125 g) butter,
    preferably salted, cut into small
    cubes and chilled
3 tablespoons all-purpose (plain)
    flour
2 cups boiling water
$^1/_4$ teaspoon coarsely ground pepper
1 tablespoon fresh lemon juice
$^1/_2$ teaspoon salt, or to taste

Melt half the butter in a saucepan over medium heat. Whisk in flour and cook, whisking, for 2–3 minutes. Gradually whisk in the boiling water, and cook, until smooth, then add pepper and lemon juice. Reduce heat to low and simmer for 5 minutes. Whisk in the remaining butter, piece by piece, until incorporated. Add salt. Serve warm.

Makes about 2 cups (16 fl oz/500 ml)

Quick ponzu

$^1/_2$ cup (4 fl oz/125 ml) soy sauce
$2^1/_2$ tablespoons fresh lemon juice

In a small bowl, combine all ingredients. Pour into individual dipping bowls. Serve the same day it is made.

Makes about $^2/_3$ cup (5 fl oz/ 150 ml)

Nuoc cham

2 small garlic cloves
2 small fresh red chilies, seeded and
    chopped
$1^1/_2$ tablespoons sugar
juice of 1 lime
$^1/_4$ cup (2 fl oz/60 ml) fish sauce
$^1/_2$ cup (4 fl oz/125 ml) water

In a mortar, mash garlic and chili together with a pestle to make a paste. Add all remaining ingredients and stir until dissolved.

Makes about 1 cup (8 fl oz/ 250 ml)

Quick Chinese mustard

¼ cup (³/₄ oz/20 g) dry (powdered) mustard

about 2 tablespoons warm water

soy sauce, to taste (optional)

Put mustard in a small bowl and gradually blend in just enough water to make a smooth paste. Let stand for 10 minutes before serving. If desired, thin with a little soy sauce. This is a very piquant sauce, and a little goes a long way.

Makes about ⅓ cup (3 fl oz/ 90 ml)

Aromatic oil marinade

2 shallots (French shallots), very finely chopped

2 garlic cloves, very finely chopped

½-inch (12-mm) piece fresh ginger, finely grated

grated zest of 1 orange

grated zest of 1 lime or lemon

a few sprigs of fresh thyme, or 1 teaspoon dried thyme

2 teaspoons coarsely ground pepper

1 teaspoon coarse salt (optional)

½ cup (4 fl oz/125 ml) olive oil

In a shallow casserole dish, combine all ingredients.

Makes about ⅔ cup (5 fl oz/ 150 ml)

Mongolian firepot dip

¾ cup (6 fl oz/180 ml) soy sauce

¼ cup (2 fl oz/60 ml) peanut oil

1 tablespoon grated fresh ginger

1 scallion (shallot/spring onion), finely chopped

2 tablespoons coarsely chopped fresh cilantro (fresh coriander)

pinch of cayenne pepper (optional)

In a small saucepan, bring soy sauce and oil to a boil over high heat. Immediately remove from heat and add ginger and onion. Let cool and pour into individual sauce dishes. Just before serving, add the cilantro and cayenne, if using.

Makes 1 cup (8 fl oz/250 ml)

Mizutaki sauce

2 eggs

¼ cup (2 fl oz/60 ml) rice vinegar

½ teaspoon dry (powdered) mustard

⅓ cup (3 fl oz/90 ml) good-quality oil such as grapeseed or cold-pressed vegetable

pinch of salt

In a blender, combine all the ingredients and process until frothy, about 5 seconds. Spoon the sauce into individual dipping bowls.

Makes 1 cup (8 fl oz/250 ml)

Korean vinegar dipping sauce

3 tablespoons sesame seeds, toasted
  (see page 72)
1/2 cup (4 fl oz/125 ml) soy sauce
2 tablespoons rice vinegar
1/2-inch (12-mm) piece fresh ginger,
  grated
pinch of sugar
pinch of cayenne pepper
1/2 scallion (shallot/spring onion),
  very finely chopped

In a mortar, lightly grind sesame seeds with a pestle. Stir in all remaining ingredients except the scallion. Immediately before serving, stir in the scallion and serve in individual dipping bowls.

Makes about 3/4 cup (6 fl oz/180 ml)

Chicken broth

1 chicken (about 3 lb/1 1/2 kg),
  preferably stewing (steamer) hen,
  whole or cut up
about 12 cups (96 fl oz/3 L) cold
  water
1/2-inch (12-mm) piece fresh ginger,
  thinly sliced
2 scallions (shallots/spring onions)
  white part only, chopped and
  washed well
1 tablespoon soy sauce

Rinse chicken well under cold running water. Put in a narrow, tall stock pot and add water to just cover the chicken. Bring to a boil over medium heat, uncovered. Skim to remove the foam. Add ginger, scallions, and soy sauce. Reduce heat to a simmer and cook for about 1 1/2 hours; strain and let cool.

Cover and refrigerate overnight. Remove and discard the congealed fat.

Makes 8–10 cups

Enriched meat stock

Blanch 1 pig's foot in boiling water for 1 minute. Drain and add to the pot with 1 lb (500 g) cubed pork shoulder. For Western dishes, add celery leaves, 1 chopped carrot, 1/2 teaspoon peppercorns, and 1 bay leaf, plus salt to taste; leave out for Asian ones.

Clarified butter

2 lb (1 kg) unsalted butter

In a double boiler over simmering water, melt butter. Remove from heat and let sit so the milk solids will settle to the bottom. Skim off any foam. Carefully pour or ladle the clear yellow liquid through a sieve lined with cheesecloth (muslin), making sure to leave all the white solids in the pan. Store in a sealed jar in the refrigerator.

Makes about 3 cups (28 oz/800 g)

Glossary

Ale: Traditionally, ale was made without hops, and therefore lacked the slight bitterness of beer. Today, there is little difference between ale and other beers. Substitute lager.

Appenzeller: One of the three most common Swiss cheeses, Appenzeller's aroma is slightly spicy, with hints of fermenting fruit. Although it may have a few large holes, they will not be as prevalent as in Emmentaler.

Beaufort: Regarded as the finest of the French Gruyère cheese family. See Gruyère and Emmentaler.

Blue: An internal-mold cheese with green-blue–colored veining. The classic blue is French Roquefort, made from sheep's milk. Other blues are commonly made from cow's milk, and more rarely goat. Although varying in taste and texture, blue cheeses are largely interchangeable in most recipes. Other notable blues include Gorgonzola from Italy, which sometimes comes blended with mascarpone; bleu de Bresse; fourme d'Ambert; English stilton; and a plethora of crumbly cow's-milk blues.

Cantal: This firm cheese could loosely be called the French version of Cheddar, although it has a delicately sour under-taste. Use interchangeably with mild to medium Cheddar.

Cellophane noodles: Commonly known as bean threads, these very thin strands are generally made from mung beans. Soak in hot to boiling water until translucent before using. Cellophane noodles can easily be discerned from rice noodles by their pliable elasticity. Brittle rice noodles break easily, while bean noodles do not.

Cheshire: A traditional English cow's-milk cheese. Like Cheddar, this was originally a cloth-wrapped cartwheel, but is now more commonly made into a rectangular shape.

Cider, hard: Fermented apple juice, not to be confused with nonalcoholic apple cider. European apple cider commonly tastes bone dry, with little or no residual sugar or fresh fruit flavor. This is the preferred style to use in fondue.

Coconut milk/cream: Canned (tinned) unsweetened coconut milk and cream is available at all Asian grocers and most supermarkets. Do not use sweetened "cream of coconut," which is specially created for desserts or alcohol drinks like piña coladas. When purchasing coconut milk and cream, note that "cream" is the thickest, "milk" is thinner, and "water" refers to the watery liquid in the center of a coconut shell. When a label fails to clearly identify the product, shake the can. The thicker it is, the less it will splash. Once home, place the can in the refrigerator and the richest portion will rise to the top; carefully spoon it off.

Colby: A washed-curd cow's-milk cheese, colby cheese originated in America but is now made world-wide. The cheese is soft and slightly elastic, and innocuously mild.

Comté: A member of the French Gruyère cheese family, Comté has pea-sized holes. See also Gruyère and Emmentaler.

Edam: Easily identifiable because of its red ball shape, Edam is usually sold young, and its texture creamy and flavor mild. Aged Edam, although rare, has a good flavor when melted.

Emmentaler: The famous holey cheese of Switzerland, Emmentaler is commonly confused with the hole-less Gruyère. Although similar, Emmentaler's aroma is sweeter, and its texture smoother and more elastic. French-made Emmental is similar.

Feta: The best and creamiest feta cheeses are made from sheep's and goat's milk; cow's-milk feta is much firmer. Feta is brined and consequently is very salty, with a distinct tang.

Fish sauce: A salty, pungent Southeast Asian seasoning made from fermented fish. It is especially popular in Thailand and Vietnam, where it is known as nam pla and nuoc mam, respectively.

Fontina: A mild and creamy cheese from Italy, fontina becomes soft at room temperature. It has the sweetness of Emmentaler and the tang of Gruyère, and a suggestion of Port-Salut. Substitute with a young version of any of those cheeses, a Tilsit, or preferably, a Fribourg vacherin.

Galangale: A rhizome related (and similar) to fresh ginger, galangale is especially popular in Thai dishes.

Gorgonzolla: See Blue.

Gouda: A Dutch cow's-milk cheese resembling a strong-tasting Edam. When young, this is a mild-tasting cheese, creamy in texture, faintly sweet and fruity. Mature Gouda, which is aged for 18 months, becomes granular and easy to grate.

Gruyère: A firm to hard cow's-cheese from Switzerland, nutty yet earthy in character. Confusingly, "Gruyère" is also generically used to describe similar French mountain cheeses such as Comté, Beaufort, and Emmental. Unlike Emmentaler and Swiss-style variants, Gruyère has no holes.

Monterey Jack: A very mild white cheese made from cow's milk. Popular in the United States, this cheese is used in Southwestern Tex-Mex dishes and Cal-Mex dishes. Substitute colby, mozzarella, or Münster.

Jarslberg: See Swiss-style cheese.

Kimchi: A Korean pickle, usually cabbage but also radish, fermented and fiery with chili.

Kirsch: A clear cherry distillate, or eau-de-vie.

Konbu: A variety of dried kelp from Japan, and an essential ingredient in the Japanese stock known as dashi. It is available in Japanese grocery stores and at select health food outlets.

Lancashire: English cow's-cheese, crumbly and mild, but sharper with age. Use as a substitute for Cheddar in Welsh rarebit.

Mascarpone: A cultured-cream, with a sweet yet slightly acidic taste. It is traditionally made from the cream skimmed during the manufacture of Parmesan cheese.

Parmesan: A hard, strong-tasting cheese used as a topping and a flavoring.

Pizza cheese: Grated cheese sold generically in supermarkets, usually a blend of one or more cheeses, such as mozzarella, colby, mild Cheddar, jack, and sometimes Parmesan. Depending on the blend—especially when there is a dominant Cheddar or Parmesan content—this cheese may prove unreliable in a fondue.

Porter: Traditionally a blend of pale beer, brown beer, and stale ale, porter is similar to stout, but not so strong. If unavailable, use stout.

Port-Salut: A semi-soft cow's-cheese with a bright orange rind. Slightly nutty, it is milder in taste than it looks. Originally, it was made by monks in France. Substitute a Chaumes or St Paulin.

Provolone: Commonly sold in large, white-waxed balls or huge cylinders, tied with a cord and hanging from a rack. This cow's-milk cheese, originally from Italy, is now widely manufactured overseas. Young provolone is mild and supple, while aged provolone has a strong, pungent flavor.

Raclette: Versions of this cow's-milk cheese, originally from the Valais, are today made abroad. Their taste is usually less well aged and distinct than that of their Swiss counterparts. Raclette cheese has a creamy consistency that melts easily but does not run. Semi-firm cheeses such as Tilsit and German-style Münster may be substituted. Raclette is also served as a table cheese.

Rice paper: Thin and brittle sheets made from rice starch. These require soaking before use. Round rice paper are known in Vietnamese as *bénh tráng*, and are available from Asian grocery stores.

Rice vinegar: A mild vinegar, especially popular in east Asia. Rice vinegar does not have as strong an acidity as Western vinegar. Do not substitute with seasoned rice vinegar, or with Chinese black vinegar, which is usually made from wheat, millet, and sorghum.

Rice wine: Chinese cooking wine is brewed from glutinous rice and millet. Japanese sake, although more expensive, may be substituted, as may dry sherry. Chinese Shaoxing wine, although made from rice, may prove too dominant in flavor, as it is well aged. Do not substitute sweetened rice wines, such as Japanese mirin.

Sapsago (Schabzieger): A hard, green-imbued cone-shaped cheese, assertive in flavor. Freshly grated Parmesan has a similar texture—but not flavor—to Sapsago, and may be substituted.

Shaoxing wine: See Rice wine.

Soy sauce: Chinese light soy sauce is similar to standard Japanese soy sauce. Do not use Chinese dark or thick soy sauce. All Japanese soy sauces in the international market are naturally brewed, not chemically manufactured.

Stout: A very dark to black beer, renowned for its creamy head. Its faintly sweet taste is countered with the bitterness of hops. The most famous brand of stout is Guinness.

Swiss-style cheese: A generic cheese only faintly resembling Emmentaler, with large holes. Generally it has little pronounced flavor, and it is available in small rectangles. A good substitute is Norwegian Jarslberg.

Tilsit: A firm cow's-milk cheese of both Dutch and German heritage. It is faintly piquant and similar in taste to Gouda, although the primary difference is its washed rind that forms into a hard crust.

Tomme, or tome: A generic term for cheese, commonly (but not exclusively) the hard mountain styles such as Beaufort. The celebrated tomme de Savoie is made from cow's milk, while a distant Pyrenees version may be sheep's milk. Both cheeses can be used in fondues.

Vacherin: Fribourg vacherin, or vacherin fribourgeois, is a creamier version of Gruyère, yet its flavor is less savory. Substitute French reblochon. The similarly named "vacherin Mont d'Or" is not interchangeable.

Index

Guide to weights and measures

The conversions given in the recipes in this book are approximate. Whichever system you use, remember to follow it consistently, thereby ensuring that the proportions are consistent throughout a recipe.

WEIGHTS

Imperial	Metric
⅓ oz	10 g
½ oz	15 g
¾ oz	20 g
1 oz	30 g
2 oz	60 g
3 oz	90 g
4 oz (¼ lb)	125 g
5 oz (⅓ lb)	150 g
6 oz	180 g
7 oz	220 g
8 oz (½ lb)	250 g
9 oz	280 g
10 oz	300 g
11 oz	330 g
12 oz (¾ lb)	375 g
16 oz (1 lb)	500 g
2 lb	1 kg
3 lb	1.5 kg
4 lb	2 kg

VOLUME

Imperial	Metric	Cup
1 fl oz	30 ml	
2 fl oz	60 ml	¼
3	90 ml	⅓
4	125 ml	½
5	150 ml	⅔
6	180 ml	¾
8	250 ml	1
10	300 ml	1¼
12	375 ml	1½
13	400 ml	1⅔
14	440 ml	1¾
16	500 ml	2
24	750 ml	3
32	1L	4

USEFUL CONVERSIONS

¼ teaspoon	1.25 ml
½ teaspoon	2.5 ml
1 teaspoon	5 ml
1 Australian tablespoon	20 ml (4 teaspoons)
1 UK/US tablespoon	15 ml (3 teaspoons)

Butter/Shortening

1 tablespoon	½ oz	15 g
1½ tablespoons	¾ oz	20 g
2 tablespoons	1 oz	30 g
3 tablespoons	1 ½ oz	45 g

OVEN TEMPERATURE GUIDE

The Celsius (°C) and Fahrenheit (°F) temperatures in this chart apply to most electric ovens. Decrease by 25°F or 10°C for a gas oven or refer to the manufacturer's temperature guide. For temperatures below 325°F (160°C), do not decrease the given temperature.

Oven description	°C	°F	Gas Mark
Cool	110	225	¼
	130	250	½
Very slow	140	275	1
	150	300	2
Slow	170	325	3
Moderate	180	350	4
	190	375	5
Moderately Hot	200	400	6
Fairly Hot	220	425	7
Hot	230	450	8
Very Hot	240	475	9
Extremely Hot	250	500	10

First published in the United States by Periplus Editions (HK) Ltd., with
editorial offices at 153 Milk Street, Boston, Massachusetts 02109 and
130 Joo Seng Road #06-01 Singapore 368357

Copyright 2001 by Lansdowne Publishing Pty Ltd.

Library of Congress Cataloging-in-Publication Data is available.

ISBN 0-7946-9001-7

Published in association with:
The American Cooking Guild
a division of Powerline Publishing Group, Inc.
Boynton Beach, Florida, USA

Set in Frutiger on QuarkXPress
Printed in Singapore

08 07 06 05 04 03   9 8 7 6 5 4 3 2